CW00369538

## About Demos

*Who we are*

Demos is the think tank for everyday democracy. We believe everyone should be able to make personal choices in their daily lives that contribute to the common good. Our aim is to put this democratic idea into practice by working with organisations in ways that make them more effective and legitimate.

*What we work on*

We focus on six areas: public services; science and technology; cities and public space; people and communities; arts and culture; and global security.

*Who we work with*

Our partners include policy-makers, companies, public service providers and social entrepreneurs. Demos is not linked to any party but we work with politicians across political divides. Our international network – which extends across eastern Europe, Scandinavia, Australia, Brazil, India and China – provides a global perspective and enables us to work across borders.

*How we work*

Demos knows the importance of learning from experience. We test and improve our ideas in practice by working with people who can make change happen. Our collaborative approach means that our partners share in the creation and ownership of new ideas.

*What we offer*

We analyse social and political change, which we connect to innovation and learning in organisations. We help our partners show thought leadership and respond to emerging policy challenges.

*How we communicate*

As an independent voice, we can create debates that lead to real change. We use the media, public events, workshops and publications to communicate our ideas. All our books can be downloaded free from the Demos website.

**www.demos.co.uk**

First published in 2005
© Demos
Some rights reserved – see copyright licence for details

ISBN 1 84180 144 5
Copy edited by Susannah Wight
Typeset and produced by Land & Unwin, Towcester
Printed in the United Kingdom

For further information and
subscription details please contact:

Demos
Magdalen House
136 Tooley Street
London SE1 2TU

telephone:  0845 458 5949
email:  hello@demos.co.uk
web:  www.demos.co.uk

# Joining Forces

From national security to networked security

Rachel Briggs

**DEMOS**

# DEM⊙S

# Contents

# Acknowledgements

I would like to thank a number of people for their ideas, help, feedback or support.

At Demos, I would like to thank Tom Bentley, Charlie Edwards, Claire Ghoussoub, Eddie Gibb, Abi Hewitt, Sam Hinton-Smith, Julia Huber and Eliza Lam, who have contributed in various ways towards making this collection a reality.

I would also like to thank the project partners who have made this work possible and, along with other colleagues, continue to offer valuable support: Bruno Brunskill at Anite Public Sector; Stephen Parkin at Astra Zeneca; John Sullivan at BP; Bruce McVean at CABE; Richard Fenning at Control Risks Group; Richard Sutton at Group 4 Falck; Karl Barclay at HSBC; Andrew Marshall at Kroll; James Thomas at Pfizer; John Smith at Prudential; and Mike Basnett at Shell.

Finally, thanks to the multitude of people who contribute to our research and attend Demos events – this type of involvement is vital to the success of our work. There are too many to name here.

Rachel Briggs
May 2005

# 1. Introduction

*The growing connectedness of the world is the most important social and economic fact of our time. It is manifest in the growth of physical links like telecom networks; in rising flows of goods, money, ideas and people; in the interconnectedness of culture and the environment; and in the new forms of social organisation.*

Geoff Mulgan, Network Logic[1]

*At a time of stability, our best asset in problem solving is our experience. But during a time of revolution, experience can be an obstacle to adapting – perhaps even nothing less than fatal baggage.*

Chris Donnelly[2]

At the dawn of the twenty-first century, it feels as if our only source of stability is the certainty that things keep changing and getting more complicated: we can't predict the future, but it's sure to be pretty messy. The reasons for this are familiar and well rehearsed. The end of the Cold War broke the global geopolitical stasis. It left a plethora of fragile nations looking for a new direction, and some old superpowers searching out new sources of strength and legitimacy. Globalisation (economic, cultural and social), the growing power of regional blocs, such as the European Union (EU), and the meteoric rise of global corporates have seen nation states reduced from principal leads to supporting actors. And the rise of the global media has not only brought news from distant shores into our front rooms, it has created a new set of expectations among societies. Publics are hungry for information and capable of making informed judgements about the decisions of their leaders.

September 11 seemed to encapsulate the security implications of this new reality: non-state terrorists fighting a cultural and religious 'war', using symbols of globalisation (aeroplanes) as weapons to take down the symbolic heart of global trade (the World Trade Center) and blow a hole through the power base of US hegemonic military power (the Pentagon), with no aspiration towards nationhood. Some have called this 'asymmetric' warfare, but that description doesn't seem to go far enough and remains rooted in the old order.

### Change on a revolutionary scale

In his now famous 2001 Labour Party Conference speech, British Prime Minister Tony Blair likened the impact of the September 11 attacks to a kaleidoscope being shaken up, with the pieces settling to create a new and entirely unfamiliar picture. We might question whether September 11 was the point of change or the moment of realisation of what had been taking place over the last decade. Regardless of the chronology, this is change on a revolutionary scale.

While the terrorists, criminals, hackers and war lords have grasped this new reality, the policy community is struggling to produce the step change needed in its response. For too long our responses to the new security environment have been piecemeal and have done nothing more than tinker around the edges. *Joining Forces* argues that the cumulative impact of the changes described constitutes revolutionary change. At such times, not only are our tried-and-tested responses and forms of organisation ineffective, but, as Chris Donnelly's quotation reminds us, our experience can be more of a hindrance than help during periods of rapid and deep-seated change.

## A piecemeal response

The UK government has recognised the need for 'joined up' thinking and doing, but the structures of Whitehall get in the way. There has been a series of initiatives aimed at achieving 'partnership' between the government and non-governmental actors, but almost all are marked by a continuing assumption – usually on both sides, to be fair – that public leads and private follows. Government attempts to increase the information available within the public domain have largely been unsuccessful: its information campaign on emergencies has been met with derision and its Iraq dossier with contempt. A recent report from the Prime Minister's Strategy Unit recognises the need for government to act preventatively rather than reactively to stem the flow of problems, but large questions remain about how to make this work in practice.

The corporate sector has also been slow to adapt to the changing nature of the global security environment. While some companies are increasing spending on security, the majority have failed to realise the strategic importance of corporate security. It is still perceived as being something that is delivered on the margins by the corporate security department or guards on doors, rather than as something which is integrated into the everyday decisions of the business. Companies on the whole have not grasped their wider responsibilities in relation to security and have failed to imagine themselves as being part of public policy discourse. The effectiveness of a company's security is not just a concern for itself. As companies become more important targets for terrorists and criminals, and take on the traditional roles of the state in some circumstances, their security is a public good.

Aid agencies are beginning to realise that as the rules of engagement in conflict zones and regions of instability have changed, they no longer have the immunity from attack that they have tended to enjoy. There are serious debates about the value of security: on the one hand agencies have a duty of care to their staff, but on the other hand highly visible security can make individuals a more attractive target. NGOs are also cautious about working in partnership on the ground, because of the danger that cooperation is perceived as being a sign that they are no longer neutral.

And while the public demands more and more information from government and public bodies, there is still patchy understanding of the crucial contribution individuals can make to the global security agenda through their everyday choices.

*Joining Forces* argues that we need to grasp the enormity of the changes we face and step up to the challenge of re-shaping and re-defining our approach to security. We need to cast aside old assumptions about roles and responsibilities; we must re-form our institutions and networks in ways that make sense of the new reality; we must radically shift mindsets to ensure we are able to understand properly the nature and complexity of the threats we face; and we must avoid the temptation to replace the current structures and norms with new ones that reflect today's reality today, but are unable to adapt at the rate at which change is now likely to happen.

In a complex, fast-paced and networked world we need a security doctrine that is fit for purpose. This is what we call *networked security*.

**Just as governments have lost their monopoly on the use of force, they must accept they no longer have a monopoly over security**

> *Analysts predict that it cost just $400,000–500,000 to plan and conduct the attacks of September 11. The attackers were able to get their money through a combination of companies, charities and international banks.*

> *The Alliance Against Counterfeit and Piracy estimates that counterfeiting and piracy cost the UK £11 billion in 2003. But in a survey of consumers, less than half of those questioned said they knew that there was a link between counterfeit and organised crime.*

*The person responsible for fatally shooting WPC Yvonne Fletcher at the Libyan People's Bureau in 1984 evaded investigation by claiming diplomatic immunity inside the embassy. Shortly after the shooting, 30 Libyan diplomats were escorted to Heathrow to catch a plane back to Libya while the British authorities looked on helplessly.*

In his seminal Demos pamphlet, *The Post Modern State and the World Order*,[3] Robert Cooper argues that stability and security are now achieved through vulnerability and openness between states, rather than the aggressive stand-off that characterised much of the twentieth century. In the face of threats from organised criminal gangs, cross-border people, arms and drugs smugglers, international terrorists, and protesters and anarchists, it is the countries that play together that stay safe together. Self-interest can only be achieved through commitment to shared interests, which is why we have seen a move towards greater cross-border cooperation in Europe in recent years, such as that provided by the Schengen Agreement.

## Government's role has been reduced from principal lead to supporting actor

Even when they work in partnership with one another, governments are not able to tackle today's security threats single-handedly. In some instances they will need to play a supporting role to companies, NGOs or even the public at large. Since the Treaty of Westphalia, when the concept of the modern nation state was born, the prizes worth fighting for have always been firmly within the gift of nation states: secrets, land, resources, people and so on. But in the new world order, there are gains to be found elsewhere.

## Private security is a public issue

Companies are an attractive target for many groups. According to the latest figures from the US State Department, 85 per cent of terrorist attacks around the world are against the private sector. A well-placed and well-timed attack on the City of London or Wall Street would not only cause economic disruption, it would result in collateral damage and breathe fear into the heart of communities much further afield. Companies are targets for organised criminals and the British Chamber of Commerce estimates that crime costs business £19 billion each year.

## NGOs no longer have immunity from attack

Even the good work of NGOs and aid agencies no longer brings them 'immunity' from attack. The security doctrine of these organisations used to be based on the assumption that reputation and relationships bring protection, while visible security makes individuals a target. However, as war has shifted from a state-to-state to sub-state affair, many of the combatant protocols that have allowed NGOs to use this approach are less frequently observed. The withdrawal of the Red Cross from Iraq was a poignant moment, and it is interesting to note that the UN has recently set up a new secretariat for personnel safety and security, led by former Metropolitan Police Assistant Commissioner Sir David Veness.

One of the biggest hurdles we face in responding to today's security threats is the fact that the threats we face no longer fit the mental maps we have created to understand and rationalise the world. Al Qaida is one of the best examples of this problem. While many have tried to characterise al Qaida in traditional terms – its global infra-structure, clear leadership, structure and form, shared aims – it is now becoming increasingly apparent that things are not that straight-forward. Al Qaida is an ideology, not a structure; there are sympathies not links across borders; motives swing between discrete political goals (regime change in Saudi Arabia), wide-ranging ambitions (an end to Western hegemony) and the resolution of long-running local battles (Jemaah Islamiyah, the group behind the Bali bombing, in Indonesia); and the means of attack range from high-tech spectaculars (September 11) to 'old school' car and truck bombs outside nightclubs and embassies (the 2003 attack on the British consulate in Turkey).

We need a security doctrine that reflects this new reality. It must be underpinned by an acknowledgement of the legitimacy of a much wider range of actors, from governments and public bodies, to companies, aid agencies and ordinary citizens. This has to rest on a new definition of what constitutes the public interest; if companies are by far the largest target of terrorism, their private responses are of public concern and in turn merit significant and sustained support from government. Of course, the involvement of a broader group of actors in the delivery of security will raise questions about when and how individuals and organisations have the right to act. We also therefore need a new structure of governance that can marry the principle of genuine partnership with proper oversight and accountability. The only way we can do this is through a networked approach to the delivery of security.

### In a networked society, effective security depends more on our ability to collaborate than on having the right 'kit'

*In 2000, a handful of peaceful fuel protesters brought Britain's roads to a standstill, left nurses and teachers stranded unable to report in for work and emptied supermarket shelves of bread and milk faster than a Tesco shelf-stacker.*

*In 2003, a virus called SARS infected over 8,000 people and killed approximately 800 people globally. As health workers in China were coming to terms with what was happening, private schools in England closed for business as head teachers and parents worried about the risk to pupils from their Asian school friends.*

*In 2000 the 'I Love You' virus, which originated in Manila, struck business and home computers around the world. It is estimated that it hit 10 per cent of UK businesses and at the time Lloyd's of London said the costs could run into millions of pounds.*

Globalisation, we are told, is bringing us all closer together; we now live in a 'global village', rather than a 'big old world'. But while this might seem far from true when we are struggling to get some sleep on a cramped long-haul flight to Thailand or Argentina, what the three examples above show us is that life is characterised by ever-increasing layers of complexity and connectivity, where real-time decision-making is crucial and the best laid plans are quickly unpicked by changing circumstances. Problems on the other side of the world can quickly become crises at home, and glitches in one system can have domino effects on other seemingly unconnected systems. The shifting boundaries between public, private and voluntary sectors are an important contributing factor, which any new security doctrine must grapple with.

Through the process of privatisation, much of what was traditionally under state control passed into private hands. For example, until the 1980s and early 1990s, the critical national infrastructure – the core services that are essential to keep the country going during an emergency: water, electricity, gas, and so on – were in the hands of the state. Today, many are part of the private sector. We have also become dependent on new services, such as electronic money transfer and information technology, which are also controlled by the private sector. What was once a relatively straightforward system now requires the coordination of many hundreds of organisations across public and private sectors and across different parts of the economy.

## States have outsourced many of their traditional responsibilities

Over the last 20 years or so, states have outsourced many of the functions they have traditionally performed, for either financial or political reasons. The fallout of the Cold War left many states fragile and weak, and as a result civil or internal wars have grown enormously. Britain, like many developed nations, provides assistance to these areas, but there is a finite limit on its resources and on the tolerance of the British public for body bags.

In countries such as Iraq and Afghanistan the use of private security companies is growing, both to protect assets and to take part in the reconstruction efforts. Debates will continue to rage about the rights and wrongs of these trends, especially the use of private military companies, following events involving companies such as Sandline and Executive Outcomes in countries such as Papua New Guinea and Angola.

In countries at risk of instability, people working for voluntary organisations are sometimes the only individuals willing to go in to provide assistance. They often find themselves in the firing line, and worry about their positioning in relation to government organisations because of their desire to appear neutral on the ground.

## Governments cannot continue to play the same role

We must stop pretending that governments can play the same role in a world where demand for their traditional services far outstrips supply. These changes are creating new and complex relationships between state and non-state actors. The controversies surrounding private military or security companies have obscured essential work carried out by non-state actors providing protection for embassies and international agencies, as well as for the hundreds of thousands of private contractors who are rebuilding the infrastructure of Iraq. According to analysts, there is one private contractor in Iraq for every ten foreign soldiers, and it is estimated that approximately 230 private contractors have so far died there, compared with 1,500 US soldiers.

Many private contractors are themselves asking for a better steer from government on how they operate and there are calls for regulation and better governance structures to be put in place. This is politically hot stuff for governments, worried about public and media reaction at home. But as the reality on the ground changes, and as we become more aware of the links between home and abroad, it is time to stop sweeping these types of 'problems' under the carpet and pretending that governments really can provide the range of services and functions they used to in a world where demand unfortunately far outstrips supply.

## Self-interest is delivered through shared interest

Collaboration will become the distinguishing factor of success for security in the future. This needs to happen on three levels. First, there need to be new structures of decision-making that allow the full range of relevant actors to participate. Naturally, checks and balance will need to be in place to ensure accountability. But until we have the types of governance structures that reflect reality, we will never manage to realise the full potential of the resources on offer.

Second, we need a shared vision of the future, where governments, companies, voluntary sector organisations and community groups scenario plan together. In a world of complexity, where the actions of one group influence others, our mechanisms of scenario planning and forecasting must be joined up, too. In reality, this will initially involve more ad hoc 'mixing' between groups, with corporate representatives being asked to take part in government scenario planning or civil servants getting involved in community group sessions. But in time we need a much more sophisticated and collaborative system.

Finally, collaboration must become a reality at an operational level. Perhaps because of the practical imperative, this is the area where there has been the greatest effort to form routes for cooperation, in some cases with considerable success. In particular, there is a growing number of examples of partnership between the public and private sectors.

Project Griffin is an initiative run jointly by the City of London and Metropolitan Police with the financial and business community to raise awareness of counter-terrorism measures among security officers in the City of London, City of Westminster, Tower Hamlets and Canary Wharf. Its aim is to ensure that security officers are better equipped to be of daily assistance to their own organisations and to the police service as well as in the event of an emergency. It is based on the assumptions that self-interest is best served through shared interest and that everyone achieves more through working together than they do on their own.

The initiative has three elements: a training day, which has now reached over 1,200 security officers; a 'bridge call' on a Friday evening to share information on the threat; and the deployment of security officers to work alongside police officers on cordon control in the event of a major incident. The value and effectiveness of this initiative are best exemplified by its record in arranging random bridge calls when specific needs have arisen (so far only twice). It was able to facilitate the calls within just 90 minutes and it is estimated that, once disseminated, over 500,000 business people were additionally supported by this sharing of information.

### It is only by joining forces that we will find effective and lasting solutions

While it is important that we ensure we have the right kit in place to respond to security problems when they arise, from stockpiling vaccines and protective clothing to making sure that police communication equipment works on the London Underground, the most important area of investment for the future must be the investment we make in partnerships and other forms of collaborative capacity. If it is only by joining forces that we find effective and lasting solutions, then the concept of partnership must underpin our approaches to security.

### Security is not something that is done to you or for you – participation is key

*Phishing is a form of online theft that uses spoofed emails, fraudulent websites and crimeware to trick consumers into divulging personal financial data. The number of phishing websites increased by 100 per cent in 2004 and last year saw a number of major attacks, including on the NatWest Bank. But in a survey for AOL UK, 84 per cent of home computer users did not know what phishing was.4 A representative from AOL UK said, 'If internet users can't understand the language used to describe these risks, they are going to find it hard to protect themselves from being ripped off.'*

> *A 2003 central government survey of terrorism preparedness at the local level found that 77 per cent of upper tier authorities and 70 per cent of police forces said they did not have plans on how to decontaminate members of the public in the event of a mass evacuation; nine out of ten police services, fire services and local authorities had no plans to deal with contaminated buildings; four out of ten councils admitted they would not be able to cope with evacuations of more than 1,000 homes; and only four out of ten police forces had trained all the officers they said they needed for emergency terrorism response teams.*[5]

Security is not something that can be delivered discretely for a country by its government, police forces or intelligence services. A security department alone cannot 'do' security for a company or organisation. While all these people and entities provide valuable input, experience and structures, they are only part of the picture. In reality, security is a participatory activity; without the active engagement of the full range of actors, security is patchy and partial.

## The growth of commitment-based security

In the private sector, there is a growing body of work on what has been termed 'commitment-based security'. It is based on the assumption that effective security in the workplace requires the commitment of everyone and must therefore be an integral part of the daily working practices of employees right across the company. In response to the growing threat of product contamination through bio-terrorism, a major US-based food processor formed an anti-terrorism task force with the goal of evaluating and updating the security needs of each of its 11 facilities. A company representative remarked about the decision to pursue commitment-based security, 'The only way to make our total security plan successful was to harness the eyes, ears, minds, spirit and support of every employee.'

As such, psychology needs to become an important component of our new security doctrine. The success of any new approach will rest on its ability to put in place systems, processes and protocols that reflect the needs and desires – rational or not – of the human beings that deliver them. Objective systems that work in theory but do not take into account the human element will not work in practice. As Briskin (1998) has observed,

> To explore the challenge to the human soul in organisations is to build a bridge between the world of the personal, subjective, and even unconscious elements of individual experience and the world of organisations that demand rationality, efficiency, and personal sacrifice . . . we must be willing to shift our viewpoint back and forth between what organisations want of people and what constitutes human complexity: the contradictory nature of human needs, desires and experience.

### Public opinion matters

Public opinion is becoming an increasingly important factor influencing the responses of companies, governments and others to security threats. While public engagement is central to any effective security policy, public perceptions rarely reflect the true nature of the risks and can as a result distract decision-makers from the genuine priorities. To counter this trend, many have argued that the amount of information available must be increased, with the assumption being that greater information will lead to a better-informed public, and eventually to better policy outcomes.

A better informed public is certainly a desirable element of a new security doctrine, but the practicalities remain problematic. There is evidence to suggest that increased flows of information can confuse rather than clarify. In some cases this can leave individuals unsure about what they should do and paralysis leads to negative outcomes.

For example, in 1998 a paper published in the *Lancet* claimed that the MMR vaccine could cause inflammatory bowel disease and autism among children. Although the research had drawn on just 12 cases, the speculation was treated as fact by sections of the media. Fearing for the worst, many parents decided not to immunise their children, despite evidence from a study of 1.8 million children in Finland, which showed no link between the vaccine and these complaints. The outcome of this panic was tangible: it left 15 per cent of British children lacking immunisation against measles, mumps and rubella, creating the possibility of a revival of these diseases.

## A culture of fear

Many have argued that MMR is not an isolated example, but symptomatic of a much wider trend: the 'culture of fear', where hype is met with yet more hype, and the result is a scared and 'paralysed' public and increasingly reactive decision-makers. If we were able to rely on governments and institutions to deliver security on our behalf, this situation would be undesirable but not disastrous. However, because effective security also requires the public to play a role, the culture of fear has implications for our capacity to respond to security threats.

There is a danger that the current 'war on terror' rhetoric could produce similar outcomes. A recent Home Affairs Select Committee looked at the impact of the 'war on terror' on community relations and found that community cohesion had been negatively affected by the current approach.[6] Communities are left divided, and this creates an immediate danger that minorities will be falsely suspected of being a threat. There is also a longer-term risk that trust – a necessary element of participation – will diminish at the local level.

## Talk is cheap – but has a lasting effect on our ability to respond

Leaders – political and non-political – must assume responsibility for initiating and maintaining sensible debates about security. Talk might be cheap, not least at election time when parties are trying to position themselves as being the only credible defence against immigration, terrorism, crime or whatever the concern of the day might be. But when these sound-bites exaggerate the risks or seek to reinforce the myth of the all-knowing, all-powerful government, this type of tactic is not only cynical. It also leaves the public feeling powerless to act, and our communities weaker as a result.

The overriding sense of fear has been exploited by politicians who have carefully re-positioned security as an area of policy where there is no room for question and debate. The stakes are so high, we are told, that we must let our politicians get on with looking after us as they see fit. This ignores not only the need to engage, but also the nature of the threats. Furthermore, there must be more honesty about the fact that there is no such thing as a straightforward 'right' answer. Information relating to security is rarely useful without analysis and judgement because of the number of variables and Rumsfeldian 'unknown unknowns'.

### At a time when 'stories' are so influential, experts have a responsibility to speak up

As an exercise in openness, the government's dossier on Iraq should be welcomed. The lesson that shouldn't be learned from the Iraq dossier is that being vocal is a bad thing. In an age where 'stories' are so influential, experts – within and outside government – have an even greater responsibility to speak up and give leadership, especially when their own opinions run contrary to public perceptions of a particular risk. But Blair's cabinet has had to learn the hard way the dangers of presenting argument as fact to a public that has a sophisticated understanding of what's going on.

### We must engage citizens as 'unlikely counter-terrorists'

We must not leave the public out of the discussions, not least because ordinary citizens have an important role to play in delivering security in a networked world. Because al Qaida tends to be talked about in terms of global networks, it is often assumed that our responses have to be suitably grandiose – nothing short of full blown war, in fact, in the case of Bush's global war on terror. But as outgoing Assistant Commissioner Sir David Veness reminded us at a recent Demos lecture, one of the most pressing challenges we face in tackling groups with sympathies towards al Qaida in the UK is working at the community level.[7] If we are to stop these loose affiliations embedding themselves and maturing into cohesive networks, we must find ways of engaging citizens and community leaders as unlikely counter-terrorists. This will not happen if citizens feel unduly scared and immobilised in the face of government 'hard talk' and posturing.

There is also a danger that we place misguided trust in technology to deliver security, forgetting that technological 'kit' is only as effective as the socio-technical systems it is employed within, and the humans operating it. The use of closed circuit television (CCTV) provides a useful example. Throughout the 1980s and 1990s, the growing risk posed by frequent and severe terrorist attacks on the mainland by the IRA and the growing fear of crime among the public caught policy-makers and politicians off guard. Around this time, CCTV was beginning to be used on private property and, despite the lack of evidence about its effectiveness, the government embarked on a massive programme to roll out coverage. John Major devoted more than three-quarters of the crime prevention budget to encourage local authorities to install CCTV and between 1996 and 1998 CCTV became the single most heavily funded non-criminal justice crime prevention measure. It is now estimated that the average Briton is photographed by more than 300 separate cameras from 30 separate CCTV networks in one day.[8] The Home Office's own recent studies have concluded that there is no evidence to suggest that CCTV reduces crime.

### We are never 'consumers' of security, only producers

Security is not something that is done to you or for you; we are never 'consumers' of security, only producers. While security has tended to be one of the most closed areas of policy, centred around the government and linked public bodies, security today is delivered by a wider range of actors and we must find ways of reflecting this in our institutions, frameworks and policies. Information is key: we need to create information flows that bring together experts and non-experts, and that allow for genuine two-way exchange as opposed to 'public information'. And this must be transacted within a public space for discussion that is open, sensible, honest and proportionate rather than based on fear and reactive decision-making. We must not underestimate the challenges of galvanising momentum at the community level. Our societies are now more fractured than they have been for a long time. It is estimated that by 2020, 40 per cent of households will be made up of people living on their own.[9]

So, for many reasons, this is not an easy vision to realise. But if we are going to match the threats with a policy framework that works, it is time to rise to the challenge of large-scale change and make this vision of networked security a full-blown reality.

## About this collection

This collection contains five reports that Demos produced within the course of the last year. They tackle aspects of the new global security agenda set out here and suggest ways in which the networked security doctrine could work in practice:

○ *Perception gap: public attitudes to security and their impact on policy-making and corporate decision-making* looks at the ways in which public perceptions of security impact on the way security is managed.

○ *Hidden assets: putting people at the heart of security* argues that security is only effectively delivered through wide-scale participation, whether within a company or organisation or at the national and international level.

○ *Next generation corporate governance: help or hindrance to effective security decision-making?* examines the impact of corporate governance and regulation on the way that companies approach security and risk taking.

○ *Beyond measure: getting the maths of security right* assesses the types of measures that can help companies to make effective decisions about security.

○ *Invisible security: the impact of counter-terrorism on the built environment* examines the ways in which counter-terrorism policies and practices are changing the face of our cities. It looks at the potential to 'design security in' and the value of engaging local communities in the fight against terrorism.

The first four reports stem from seminars run as part of a series looking at the challenges for companies of doing business in the new global security environment. The seminars were kindly supported by donations from a number of companies: Anite Public Sector, Astra Zeneca, BP, Control Risks Group, Group 4 Falck, HSBC, Kroll Security International, Pfizer, Prudential and Shell.

The final report was commissioned by the Commission for Architecture and the Built Environment (CABE) and is reproduced here with their permission as part of Demos' open access publishing policy. Demos would like to acknowledge CABE for its support of this piece of work.

# 2. Perception gap

## Public attitudes to security and their impact on policy-making and corporate decision-making

### Overview

Public opinion is becoming an increasingly important factor influencing the responses of companies and governments to security threats. While public engagement is central to any effective security policy, public perceptions rarely reflect the real nature of the risks and so can distract decision-makers from genuine priorities and result in disproportionate responses. To counter this trend, many have argued for the need to increase the amount of information available, with the assumption being that greater information will lead to a better-informed public and eventually to better policy outcomes.

This is problematic. First, there is evidence to suggest that the increased flows of information can confuse rather than clarify and may even contribute to the growing feeling of fear within many societies. Second, it assumes that there is always a straightforward 'right' answer. Information relating to security is rarely useful without analysis and judgement because there are so many variables and, in the words of Donald Rumsfeld, 'unknown unknowns'. Third, and related to this, in an age where 'stories' are so influential experts have a responsibility to speak up and give leadership, especially when their own opinions run contrary to public perceptions of a particular risk. Companies and security organisations form part of this expert group, and it is not surprising therefore that there is growing interest among the public and the media in their views. There are of course disincentives and cultural barriers to companies engaging in public or semi-public discussions about security, but it is vital that they work out how to engage as the costs of not doing so could be even higher than staying silent.

This perception gap will not go away, especially in the current climate where there is fear among the public about low probability/ high impact risks, such as terrorism. But the gap could be narrowed if expert rather than non-expert voices led public debates. It is time for companies and security organisations to find their voices. They must also renegotiate the terms of their relationship with the media from one that is conducted reluctantly and at arm's length to a positive two-way partnership.

## Public perceptions of security

Public debates about security have been on a roller coaster in recent years. In the late 1980s and 1990s fear of crime and concerns about transnational organised criminal networks dominated. Towards the end of the 1990s attention shifted towards information security and the fear that our computers would not make it into the new millennium. In the aftermath of 9/11, terrorism went from being a low salience issue to a talking point for governments, companies and individuals around the world. As more attacks failed to materialise in the West, many began to think that the events in New York and Washington had been a blip and that terrorism was something that happened away from home, and should therefore not be such an immediate priority after all (the now infamous cover story on the *Spectator* magazine the day before the Madrid bombings was an untimely pronouncement of this stance). Bombs in Istanbul and Madrid provided a timely wake-up call. Iraq distracted us, first because of fears about weapons of mass destruction falling into the hands of rogue states and terrorists, and then because it reminded us of the continuing tensions across the Middle East and the rest of the Muslim world. More recently, security fears in the UK have been directed towards immigrants, fuelled by the language of the 2005 election campaign.

The most important lesson to be drawn from the shifts in public discourse about security in recent years is that public perceptions tend to be at odds with the real nature of the risks. Academic Paul Slovic argues that people tend to make judgements about risk based on emotional feelings and intuitions about whether something is good or bad rather than a dispassionate calculation of costs and benefits.[10] He calls this the *affect heuristic*, explaining that judgements are holistic rather than analytic, they focus on pleasure and pain rather than logic, and on free associations rather than on deductive connections. In particular he highlights the importance of images, metaphors and narratives in shaping perceptions. Given the graphic nature of some of the media reporting of security risks in recent years, and the arrival of 24/7 news coverage beamed directly into our living rooms, it is not surprising that individuals worry about the risk of terrorism despite the fact that the risk of dying in a terrorist attack is dwarfed many times over by more mundane and ordinary risks of death on the road or in the home.

Many academics and scholars have argued that there is a tendency for individuals to assume that an event is more likely to recur if it is easy to remember. While the massive spread of global media means we are now more often exposed to highly graphic and visual reporting of security incidents, the relationship between images and risk perception is not entirely mediated by the media. Over one hundred years ago, Gustave Le Bon wrote his seminal text, *The Crowd*, which explored the workings of the public mind.[11] Writing before the advent of the television and the radio, he found that crowds tend to make judgements about risks based on visual images rather than on reasoned arguments, and that this means they tend to overestimate the probability of especially dramatic risks. Nobel Prize winners Amos Tversky and Daniel Kahnemann have called this the *availability heuristic*.[12] A contemporary example of this in Western societies is offered by the steadily growing fear among parents of child abduction, despite the fact that abductions have remain at approximately the same level for over 40 years.

There is evidence to suggest that the way the broadcast and print media report certain risks has exaggerated this trend. A study of prime-time television viewing in the US by George Gerbner, former dean of the Annenberg School of the University of Pennsylvania, found that heavy TV watchers are more likely than lighter ones to overestimate their chances of being involved in violence, to believe that their neighbourhood is unsafe, to say that fear of crime is a very serious problem, to assume that crime is rising even when it is falling, and to buy locks, watchdogs and guns for protection.[13] Jason Ditton of the University of Sheffield notes that 45 per cent of crimes reported in newspapers in the UK involve sex or violence, compared with only 3 per cent of reported crime.[14] When people were interviewed about how many crimes involve sex or violence, they tended to overestimate it by a factor of three and people fear being assaulted or raped more than being robbed, even though there is a higher incidence of robbery than rape.

W Kip Viscusi argues that these trends are becoming so pronounced that many people now have a *zero risk mentality*,[15] naively believing that it is possible to eliminate risks that can never entirely be eliminated, and people such as Bill Durodié and Frank Furedi argue that on both an individual and also a systemic level we are becoming increasingly risk averse. Ironically, this is happening at a time when there are signs that individuals and societies are more resilient than ever before: after the 9/11 attacks the Dow Jones recovered in less than one month. A number of studies have shown that individuals become more resilient when confronted with a disaster, with one indicator of this being a fall in suicide levels after incidents such as 9/11; there was broad agreement during discussions at the seminar (see below) that the recovery phases of disasters are getting steadily shorter over time; and a study from Oxford Metrica has shown that many companies come out of disasters much more resilient and, if managed effectively, a disaster can improve their medium-term business performance.[16]

## Public perceptions – impact on policy

Public opinion is an important factor influencing the formation of policy by both governments and private organisations. It is of course impossible to measure the extent of its impact, but a relationship can be observed. This is not surprising given that governments and companies have a duty to be accountable to their electorate and stakeholders, which obliges them to listen to their concerns. Decision-makers are also themselves part of this 'public' and cannot be expected to leave their own fears at the office door. Two examples below do not seek to prove a direct causal relationship, but do offer an interesting insight into the influence of public opinion on public policy: the massive proliferation of CCTV within the UK despite its lack of proven credentials as a crime deterrent; and the US government's exaggerated reaction to the anthrax scare in the autumn of 2001.

*CCTV*

Throughout the 1980s and 1990s, fear of crime among the public increased substantially. The growing visibility of persistent poverty and degradation in many inner city areas, an alcohol-fuelled 'yob culture', a drug-induced crime wave and the rise of sensational media reporting of these and other issues, such as child abduction, paedophilia and violent crime, left many people fearing Britain was in the middle of a crime epidemic, despite the fact that this was not always borne out by the figures. Arguably the most important influence on the public was the increasing frequency and severity of terrorist attacks on the mainland by the IRA.

At the same time, a new technology was coming of age that promised a potential solution – closed circuit television. It was already beginning to be used on private property, such as in shops, but there was hope that it could also help to tackle problems in public spaces, too. The programme of CCTV development started under the last Conservative government and was keenly continued by the Labour government when it came into office in 1997. John Major devoted more than three-quarters of the crime prevention budget to encourage local authorities to install CCTV and between 1996 and 1998 CCTV became the single most heavily funded non-criminal justice crime prevention measure. What started on a small scale in

London to protect against terrorist attacks quickly spread out to the rest of the country. It is now estimated that the average Briton is photographed by more than 300 separate cameras from 30 separate CCTV networks in one day. This investment was made without any evidence about the effectiveness of CCTV in either preventing crime or increasing the level of detection and successful prosecution. In fact, a recent study commissioned by the Home Office has found that CCTV does not result in any measurable decrease in terrorism or crime. But successive research and polling show that the public *feels* safer because of the presence of CCTV and continues to pressure local government for further expansion.

*Anthrax*

The anthrax scare in the US in 2001 is a good example of *contagion* and the influence of public opinion on public policy. Four letters containing anthrax were mailed to congressional and media leaders in October 2001, resulting in 23 cases of anthrax infection and five deaths by the end of November 2001. Unsurprisingly, this generated panic among the American public so soon after the attacks of 9/11. The government's response was rapid and extreme: the Hart Senate Office was closed for months and decontaminated at a cost of $22 million; after traces were found in the US Supreme Court it was evacuated for the first time since it was built in 1935; and when traces of spores were found at more than 20 off-site mail facilities, mail to all federal government offices was shipped to Ohio to be decontaminated, delaying its delivery for months. The US Paymaster General told Congress that the total cost of the anthrax attacks could exceed $5 billion (equivalent to $1 billion per life lost). It would be impossible for any country, even the US with its vast resources, to sustain this level of response for any length of time.

These and many other examples raise questions about the role of the expert in influencing perceptions of security risks. Talking about this dilemma in relation to science, Bill Durodié has observed that, 'The precautionary principle has the consequence of emphasising worst case scenarios, thereby encouraging a tendency to overreact to events and, most insidiously, elevating public opinion over professional expertise and subordinating science to prejudice.' It is important that similar open discussions are had in relation to security to ensure that future policy responses to security threats are informed by expert judgement rather than public fear.

## Bridging the gap

Given the existence of this relationship between public perceptions of security risks and decision-making, it is important that the perception gap is narrowed as much as possible. Participants at the seminar identified two key factors – a better evidence base and stronger leadership from experts – to counter any disproportionate responses to potential risks.

### Building the evidence base

Good and wide-ranging evidence is the bedrock of sound decision-making, but there is broad agreement within the security community that not enough good quality information is available. Many corporate security professionals instead base their judgements on years – even decades – of experience of what does and does not work and have developed informal networks to allow them to draw on a range of experiences and approaches. This may meet their own day-to-day needs, but it makes it difficult for them to transfer what they know beyond their own departments and take part in more open and public dialogue.

Given that most decisions about security are made by non-security experts, it is vital that channels be found for this information to flow more easily. As we have seen, worried publics put pressure on their political leaders to react to certain events; the Prime Minister rather than the Joint Intelligence Committee takes us into war; the effectiveness of workplace security systems relies on staff adhering to the rules; and boards rather than corporate security departments make the really big decisions about security resources and priorities within a company.

Security is not an activity that lends itself to neat statistical analysis. There are infinite numbers of variables at play; many important factors cannot be measured or are even what Donald Rumsfeld would call 'unknown unknowns'; some security risks, such as kidnapping in certain countries, are so low that even complete statistical sets would be almost meaningless but their impacts are so high they still need to be managed; and trends can move so quickly that historical information can be at best worthless (and in some cases misleading) in helping to determine future decisions.

One way to counter some of these problems would be for more organisations to pool the data and information they do have, in order to increase the reliability of their figures. But there is, perhaps understandably, caution about doing this as breaches in information security could increase operational and reputational risks. Some information providers are concerned about any resulting legal liabilities they might face by the advice they give. Another possible solution would be to record and cross-reference qualitative forms of data and information. Given what we know about the way individuals process information about risks – visually and emotionally rather than analytically – information in this format might even be more effective in communicating with non-security experts.

### Stronger leadership from experts

The media undoubtedly plays an important role in influencing public perceptions of security, but it cannot be expected to shoulder the blame alone. One of the reasons there has been an acceleration of the trends that this report discusses is because there has been a stark absence of security experts willing to take part in public discussions about security. This has meant that non-security experts have set the tone of debates and their perceptions and assumptions have been allowed to go unchecked. It is vital that companies, government departments and security organisations step forward.

This is particularly challenging for the security community, which is traditionally one of the most secretive and closed groups, which operates on a strictly 'need-to-know' basis. Those who are cautious about stepping forward will take little comfort from the mauling that the government and intelligence agencies have had as a result of the attempt to open up such discussions relating to the case for war in Iraq. The risk of reputational damage caused by ineffective communication or the growing threat of litigation may mean there are too few reasons for many to break this mould.

While such caution is understandable, security experts must be bold and resist the temptation to enter into debates from a comfortable distance. Trust is not built by being 'right', it is built by being open. Just as in personal relationships, trust between the public and individuals or organisations comes by being open and being prepared to be vulnerable and not hiding behind protocol, statistics or official positions. In time, this trust can then be converted into a currency of goodwill, which can be cashed in at more difficult times, as exemplified by the fallout from the Hutton Report. While Hutton systematically and forensically cleared it of any wrongdoing, the government had underestimated the amount of goodwill the BBC had built up with the public and still managed to come out of the episode as the bruised party. Security experts must resist the temptation to see the media as being something to control and instead seek to forge a more meaningful and open relationship based on mutual trust and respect.

## Lessons for companies

This report suggests a number of lessons for companies:

○ Companies must take seriously their responsibilities to be part of public debates about security.
○ Companies must invest in building stronger evidence on which to base their decisions, but must ensure this contains a variety of information types.
○ Security professionals must remember that decisions are rarely based on 'facts' alone; it is important they understand the role of emotions and instincts in influencing the decision-making process.

## Suggested further reading

The following books and articles expand on some of the arguments made in this report.

Adams, J, *Risk*. London: Routledge, 1995.

Flynn, J, Slovic, P and Kunreuther, H (eds), *Risk, Media and Stigma: Understanding public challenges to modern science and technology*. London: Earthscan, 2001.

Friedman, LM, *Total Justice*. New York: Russell Sage Foundation, 1994.

Gerbner, G, 'Violence and terror in and by the media' in M Raboy and B Dagenais (eds), *Media, Crisis and Democracy*. London: Sage, 1992.

Le Bon, G, *The Crowd: A study of the popular mind*. Mineola, NY: Dover Publications, 2002.

Kip Viscusi, W, 'Alarmist decisions with divergent risk information', *Economic Journal* 107, 1997, p 1657.

Raboy, M and Dagenais, B (eds), *Media, Crisis and Democracy: Mass communication and the disruption of social order*. London: Sage Publications, 1992.

Rosen, R, *The Naked Crowd: Reclaiming security and freedom in an anxious age*. New York: Random House, 2004.

Sunstein, CR, 'The laws of fear: the perception of risk', *Harvard Literature Review* 115, 2002, pp 1119, 1128–9.

Tversky, A and Kahneman, D, 'Availability: a heuristic for judging frequency and probability', *Cognitive Psychology* 5, 1973, p 207.

Welsh, BC and Farringdon, DP, *Crime Prevention Effects of Closed Circuit Television: A systematic review*, Home Office Research Study 252. London: Home Office, 2002.

This report draws on discussions at a Demos seminar held on 11 May 2004. Speakers at the seminar were **Ian Hargreaves**, group director of corporate and public affairs at BAA and former editor of the *New Statesman* and the *Independent*; **Bill Durodié**, director of the

International Centre for Security Analysis at King's College London; **Graham Minter**, deputy head of the Economic Policy Department at the FCO; and **Aldwin Wight**, chairman of Kroll's Security Consulting Group for Europe, Middle East and Africa.

The seminar was part of a series supported by donations from a number of companies: Anite Public Sector, Astra Zeneca, BP, Control Risks Group, Group 4 Falck, HSBC, Kroll, Pfizer, Prudential and Shell.

# 3. Hidden assets

## Putting people at the heart of security

**Overview**

*To explore the challenge to the human soul in organisations is to build a bridge between the world of the personal, subjective, and even unconscious elements of individual experience and the world of organisations that demand rationality, efficiency, and personal sacrifice…we must be willing to shift our viewpoint back and forth between what organisations want of people and what constitutes human complexity: the contradictory nature of human needs, desires and experience.*

Briskin, 1998

As this quote suggests, it is now commonly understood in the business world that objective systems do not alone make great companies. A company's ability to operate effectively also rests on its ability to put in place systems, processes and protocols that reflect the needs and desires – rational or not – of the human beings that staff them.

Corporate security has risen up the corporate agendas of many companies in recent years. As a result of this, and the growing appreciation that security cannot be delivered discretely by one department, corporate security departments are looking for ways to extend their reach across the company. In doing so, many are beginning to realise that the secret of effective corporate security rests less on their technical expertise (though this is clearly still important), and more on their ability to respond to the human complexities that the quotation above describes.

There are four important elements of what might be termed 'commitment-based security': corporate culture, creating ownership, going beyond a one-size-fits-all approach, and cultural sensitivity. Of course, such cross-organisational strategies are never easy to implement in practice. But the ability of corporate security departments to operate on this basis will not only enable them to create effective security policies and practices; it will also allow a department that has traditionally been at the margins of corporate life to influence business norms and change the ways their companies are led and managed.

## The rise of corporate security

In many large companies, security has assumed a much greater profile than at any time in recent history. In a 2003 survey of the members of the International Security Management Association (ISMA), which are drawn from global 200 and Fortune 500 companies, there was overwhelming consensus that business continuity and personnel safety have been propelled back to the top of the risk management agenda. This is commonly explained with reference to 9/11; in a survey carried out by Janusian of individuals responsible for corporate security in companies in Britain, two-thirds of respondents had seen their budgets rise since 9/11.[17]

But 9/11, and the ongoing threat from global terrorism and the fear this has engendered, do not alone explain this shift; a number of additional factors are playing an important role. First, as the next chapter, 'Next generation corporate governance', explains, the growth of corporate governance over the last five to ten years has created a more overt framework of responsibility at the board level. The penalties for getting security wrong are so much greater: with the introduction of the crime of corporate manslaughter and the growing trend towards personal accountability, board directors could find themselves personally liable when something goes wrong. The rise of litigation is particularly important in corporate terms because it brings not only the risk of direct financial loss, but also reputational damage, the consequences of which can last for years, as outlined in the chapter 'Perception gap'.

Second, as security becomes more visible, there are positive cumulative effects for those corporate security professionals who manage their new-found status effectively. Whereas security has tended to be considered nothing more than a drain on resources, security professionals should present its contribution to the competitive advantage of the company. For, when security is managed effectively, it allows the company to take risks with a much greater degree of certainty and can therefore be an important facilitator of new business development.

The growing prominence of security is beginning to offer corporate security professionals the opportunities to challenge business norms and change the way their companies are led and managed.

## Commitment-based security

Commitment-based security has emerged in response to these trends and offers a useful framework within which corporate security professionals can play an active role in shaping the next stage of organisational and cultural development within their companies. It is based on the assumption that security is best delivered as an integral part of the daily working practices of employees right across the company rather than being delivered discretely by the corporate security department. As such, the corporate security department's ability to link into and form trusted relationships with the rest of the organisation and the strength of its profile become as important – if not more so – as the technical skills that have dominated in the past. Commitment-based security is concerned not so much with moving security up the corporate ladder or getting greater access to the board and senior managers, but is instead focused on changing the culture across the organisation.

### Elements of a successful commitment-based security strategy

There are a number of important elements of a successful commitment-based security strategy, in particular corporate culture, creating ownership, going beyond a 'one-size fits-all' approach and cultural sensitivity.

*Corporate culture*

The most important factor influencing the ability of a company to adopt a commitment-based security strategy is its ability to motivate its staff to play an active role in delivering the security strategy in practice. Ultimately, this is determined by the corporate culture; companies need to create an environment where there is a sense of belonging and unity, a family culture where the instinct to 'protect and defend' is triggered in the minds of employees right across the organisation. It is only when individuals have a sense of how they fit into the broader scheme of things that they feel compelled to go the extra mile in delivering on their responsibilities.

Corporate culture is not static; it shifts over time in response to people and personalities, the external environment and wider trends. There are specific ways in which companies can change their cultures. Business psychologists have identified four conditions that enable employees to feel motivated enough to go beyond their job role: meaningfulness, psychological safety, enjoying positive relationships with supervisors, and psychological availability.

*Meaningfulness* Individuals have a primary motive to seek *meaningfulness* in their work, seeing the value of the purpose of their work in relation to their own sense of value. If it is not present it can lead to individuals having a sense of isolation and feeling of 'disengagement' with the work. Employees are more likely to feel involved through job enrichment, for example enabling them to work in other teams, add to their portfolio of skills, and link with other parts of the organisation. Encouraging individuals to be part of the organisation's security strategy, especially during times of heightened fears and anxieties, could feed into this process.

Individuals need to work in roles that they identify with and feel they can contribute to, beyond the normal day-to-day activities; in other words, their need to achieve a good *work role fit*. This means that corporate security departments must work hard to ensure employees have a good sense of the risks they are involved in managing, why they are critical to the future of the business and what they are individually expected to do.

The quality of *co-worker relationships* is important in making individuals feel they are being treated with dignity and respect and that their contributions are valued. Trusted relationships also allow individuals to admit when they have made mistakes without fear of personal reprisal, and in such a way that allows them to be part of the solution.

*Psychological safety* Creating a culture where employees are able to be themselves without fear of negative consequences is important for the effective delivery of a commitment-based security strategy. It is only when individuals feel safe – when situations are not ambiguous, unpredictable or threatening – that they understand the boundaries of acceptable behaviour. This ensures that they focus on what others expect of them rather than merely doing what they believe to be the 'right' thing.

*Supervisor relationship* The relationship with one's immediate manager can have a dramatic impact on an individual's perception of the safety of a work environment. A supportive manager who gives positive feedback, encourages employees to voice concerns, develop new skills and solve work-related problems engenders a sense of self-determination, and choice in regulating their own actions. To gain trust a manager must behave with consistency and integrity, share and delegate control, communicate openly and demonstrate concern for the individual. These qualities of management are all critical to delivering a commitment-based approach to security.

*Psychological availability* An individual is only able to give of themselves fully at work – and make contributions beyond their immediate daily work – if they have a strong self-belief in their professional capabilities. This works on three levels. *Physically*, they must be able to cope with their work; *emotionally*, the demands of the job should be met with emotional support from managers; and *cognitively* – where their tasks require much more information processing than an individual can handle, which can lead to them feeling overwhelmed with the number of 'balls in the air' – time must be created for them to think more clearly.

This analysis of the role of corporate cultures in shaping employee engagement suggests a number of consequences for commitment-based security strategies:

○ Security can help to create a sense of community within a company – it is underpinned by common messages, it is a shared project, there is a clear sense of how the interests of the company are aligned with the interests of individual members of staff.
○ Security departments must explain why security matters and how individuals can play a role.
○ Security departments must clearly communicate how the company's purpose relates to security.
○ Security departments must encourage non-security staff to initiate contact with the security department and show their input is being taken seriously.
○ Trusted relationships are essential.
○ The company must avoid a 'name and blame' culture when things go wrong.
○ Security departments must actively manage perceptions of security among staff.
○ Security departments must find ways of actively engaging non-security staff in shaping the strategy.
○ Security departments must not overload employees with information, or present it in a way that will not make sense to non-security professionals.

*Creating ownership*
Corporate culture needs to create the right 'tone' to encourage individuals to take ownership of security. Alongside this, there are a number of practical things that security departments can do to encourage wider buy-in.

*The board and senior management*   Getting the commitment of the board and senior management is incredibly important as their behaviour will determine corporate priorities and send out strong messages to the rest of the company and stakeholders. There are three important elements to this. First, it is important to *de-mystify security risks*. Senior managers often do not have experience in the security field and will therefore not be able – or interested – in engaging security professionals on this level. The challenge for those in the corporate security department is to present what they know in ways that are appropriate to the knowledge, skills and priorities of senior executives, and this will almost certainly require them to link security into business objectives.

Second, *security professionals must be able to illustrate effective judgement* about the nature and scale of the security risks faced by the company and the level of its vulnerabilities and potential losses. There is concern in some parts of the security world about the apparent failure of security departments to defend their assessments with data on threats, risks, vulnerabilities and responses. But as the chapter 'Beyond measure' points out there is disagreement about the extent to which this is a limiting factor, with many believing that quantification is a red herring that will prevent security managers making progress in other areas. Third, there is broad consensus that a *workshop-based approach* is the most effective format for engaging senior management.

*Employees*   It is critical that the security department finds ways to attract the attention and buy-in from staff across the company. There are a number of ways of doing this. First, it is important to *adopt a bottom-up approach*. For instance, security could work in partnership with the human resources department to ensure that all new recruits are briefed on security when they arrive and to enable security professionals to be involved in the induction process. This can be incredibly effective, but in large companies presents challenges relating to scale.

Second, security departments should *second-guess the concerns of the workforce and be proactive in addressing them in a sensitive way*. One corporate security professional at the seminar gave a personal anecdote: his department had been concerned that the screening of a television programme on the threat of a biological terrorist attack in London would create panic among the workforce. He organised for each employee to receive a short briefing note the morning after the programme explaining the company's thoughts on the scenario presented and the company's contingency plans in the event of such an attack. What could have been a crisis was averted, and the security department was able to raise its profile in the process and strengthen trust among the rest of the company.

Third, it is important that the security department seeks to *build trusted relationships across the organisation*. One way of doing this is to create informal settings within which other departments can get to know the team, learn a bit more about their work and exchange ideas about the security strategy. Many corporate security professionals do this in social events, whenever possible.

*The wider corporate 'family'*  One of the biggest unresolved questions relating to commitment-based security is how companies apply the principles of this approach to their 'extended family' of suppliers, contractors, partners, subsidiaries, and so forth. Given the distributed model of business operations that most companies adopt, the engagement of these external actors is also important, but currently under-explored.

*Beyond a 'one-size-fits-all' approach*
Inherent to a commitment-based approach to security is a rejection

of the notion that there is such a thing as 'best' practice. While such a strategy must be underpinned by a set of carefully defined principles, the way in which they are translated into practices, systems and protocols within an organisation will differ greatly from company to company. On a micro level, companies must also ensure that a good level of flexibility for different personality types is incorporated into the system they adopt. 'Leaders' will respond differently from 'followers', who will respond differently from 'risk-takers', and so forth. Command and control systems will therefore not deliver results, and instead companies need to work to enhance the adaptive capacity of their management systems.[18]

*Cultural sensitivity*

Multinational companies must be sensitive to cultural differences and how they affect their ability to implement a commitment-based approach to security. A number of factors could be important. First, risk perceptions may be geographically based. For instance, in the light of 9/11 there is much evidence to suggest that Americans are more concerned about security than their counterparts in Europe or the Middle East. Anecdotal evidence from the seminar suggested that companies are currently finding it easier to implement these strategies in the United States. Second, attitudes to hierarchy may differ between regions. For example, there is a very low tradition in Japan of individuals taking responsibility at a low level within the organisation. It might therefore be more difficult to encourage Japanese workers to engage with such policies. Companies must find ways to adapt their approaches in response to these factors.

**The limits to commitment-based security**

Like any corporate strategy, there are a number of factors that potentially limit the effectiveness of commitment-based security. Perhaps the most important challenge is *maintaining momentum* for such a diffused process, where ownership is shared across hundreds or even thousands of employees. This makes the leadership role of the corporate security department particularly important, and it is also essential that it identifies a number of leaders and catalysts from other departments who can reinforce the message more frequently.

Of course, the diffused model of management is nothing new to the corporate world. In fact, employees are now expected to be involved in the delivery of a number of core corporate functions that used to be centralised. There is therefore a *danger that individuals are being asked to juggle so many different roles that there will be resistance from some to take responsibility for anything else.* This also means that individuals are receiving information from a number of different directions from within and outside the company. Corporate security departments must therefore find ways to get their message heard in such an *overcrowded information marketplace.*

Finally, the strength of commitment-based security could also be its Achilles heel. *Many of the components are so obvious and commonsense – but not commonplace – that they can be difficult to implement.*

## Lessons for companies

This report suggests a number of lessons for companies:

○ The growing profile of security offers corporate security departments the opportunity to challenge business norms and change the way their companies are led and managed.

○ Commitment-based security offers a practical framework for this change.

○ Corporate security departments need to concentrate as much on their relationships with colleagues across the company as their technical skills.

○ Corporate security departments need to develop a clear message about how security fits within the corporate narrative and business priorities.

○ It must be clear how individuals can play a role.

○ Getting buy-in across the company is key.

○ A one-size-fits-all approach will not work. The strategy

must reflect the nuances of the company, and the needs of individuals within it.

O   The only underlying principle of best practice is flexibility or adaptability.

O   The corporate security department must identify leaders or 'champions' for security across the company.

## Suggested further reading

The following books and articles expand on or complement some of the arguments made in this report:

Armor Group, *Securing the Knowledge Enterprise*, 2001.

Belgard Group, 'Commitment based security', 2002 (available to download from www.belgard.com).

Bentley, T and Wilsdon, J (eds), *The Adaptive State: Strategies for personalising the public realm*. London: Demos, 2003 (available to download free of charge from www.demos.co.uk).

Bown, N, Read, D and Summers, B, *The Lure of Choice*. London: LSE, Department for Operational Research, 2002.

Cendant Mobility, 'New approaches to global mobility: new challenges and issues relating to cross-border transfer activity', Benchmark Study, 2002.

Chapman, J, *System Failure: Why governments must learn to think differently*. London: Demos, 2004 (available to download free of charge from www.demos.co.uk).

Power, M, *The Risk Management of Everything: Rethinking the politics of uncertainty*. London: Demos, 2004 (available to download free of charge from www.demos.co.uk).

'The power of commitment: leveraging your employees to help manage risks', *Trendline* 6, Dec 2002.

Royston-Lee, D, 'Engaging the hearts, heads and minds of employees' (this short note was prepared by David for this Demos seminar; his paper is available to download from www.demos.co.uk).

Webley, S and More, E, *Does Business Ethics Pay? Ethics and financial performance*. London: Institute of Business Ethics, 2003.

This report draws on discussions at a Demos seminar on 23 September 2004. Speakers at the seminar were **Richard Fenning**, chief operating officer at Control Risks Group; **Jamie Jemmeson**, head of security at Deutsche Bank; and **David Royston-Lee**, managing director of Partners in Flow.

The seminar was part of a series supported by donations from a number of companies: Anite Public Sector, Astra Zeneca, BP, Control Risks Group, Group 4 Falck, HSBC, Kroll, Pfizer, Prudential and Shell.

# 4. Next generation corporate governance

## Help or hindrance to effective security decision-making?

### Overview

Over the past decade, the reputation of the business community has taken quite a knocking. High profile crises and scandals – from Brent Spa and Barings to Enron and WorldCom – have undermined trust in companies. In a 2002 Mori poll, just 25 per cent of UK respondents said they would trust business leaders to tell the truth, compared with 91 per cent for doctors and 85 per cent for teachers. The prevailing wisdom that has emerged – that companies should not be left to their own devices – has brought a tide of new measures aimed at opening up their decision-making to scrutiny from outside and oversight from within. 'Corporate governance' is now common currency in boardrooms around the world and has become one of the most important defining principles for decision-making in the business community in recent history.

The jury is still out on whether corporate governance will be a help or hindrance for companies in managing their security risks. On the one hand, some security professionals report greater buy-in from colleagues within a corporate culture that values responsible and pro-active management of potential risks. On the other hand, some question whether heightened scrutiny will erode the trust that is so central to effective security management, or perpetuate the myth that all risks can be managed away. Getting this balance right is crucial. The security profession must rise to the challenge and play a full and active role in shaping the corporate governance agenda in ways that will enhance rather than limit their ability to make the right decisions for their companies and encourage commitment from all corners of their company.

## The rise of corporate governance

The past decade has witnessed a massive rise in corporate governance activity. During this time corporate governance codes have been published in 43 countries, the OECD has published a set of principles and the World Bank and IMF have produced their own guidelines, too. In the UK, the movement took off in the early 1990s with the establishment of the Cadbury Commission and the publication of its report in December 1992, followed in regular succession by other similar initiatives, including Greenbury, Hampel, Smith and Higgs. One of the most important interventions has been the Turnbull Report, which was intended to encourage best practice. Publicly traded companies are now required to report on their risks and outline risk management strategies in their annual reports, and as part of this management boards should be fully aware of the risks their company faces and the steps being taken to minimise exposures. The proportion of larger UK companies with explicit ethics policies has risen in the past ten years, from one-third to more than a half.

The rise in regulation, regulated self-regulation, guidelines, protocols and codes of best practice is in part a response to a series of high-profile, high-impact corporate failures that have undermined trust in companies. The proportion of UK citizens who say they have faith in corporations has plummeted, from two to one in favour in 1970 to two to one against today. In a 2002 Mori poll on the types of people we trust to tell the truth, only 25 per cent of respondents said they would trust business leaders, compared with 91 per cent and 85 per cent who said they would generally trust doctors and teachers. Interestingly, politicians fared worse than business leaders, earning the trust of only 19 per cent of those questioned.

### Corporate governance: a helpful tool for effective security management?

Given events in recent years, there is broad consensus within the business community that some form of oversight is useful, although exactly what that should look like in practice remains contested. As companies become increasingly aware of how security risks affect their ability to operate, security and corporate governance are likely to converge. In some companies this is already the case, and many argue that managing security within a governance framework has been helpful in securing compliance from colleagues at the top of the organisation and raising its profile within the company alongside other forms of corporate risk. As one business executive with responsibility for security commented at the seminar:

> *Have corporate governance developments helped security decision-making? Yes, they have helped. When we created our corporate governance package we didn't have to write new policies because we already had good ones in place. The problem at that stage was getting people to comply with them. It now works extremely well. The policies are now more visible at senior levels than they were previously. I get a greater level of assurance than I was doing before.*

Corporate governance has helped to create a culture that supports the furtherance of good and best practice, where information about the most effective types of behaviours, processes, structures, and protocols is shared. This is a familiar and, in many cases, essential, part of security management. Security professionals within companies often describe what they do as being 'non-competitive' and rely on regular contact and intelligence pooling with peers in competitor companies in order to get their jobs done. Because much of this activity happens 'behind closed doors', it remains to be seen whether the next generation of corporate governance developments will result in a culture clash between the security department and the boardroom.

### Corporate governance: hindrance rather than help?

As understanding of the impact of corporate governance on corporate security is beginning to deepen, concerns are being voiced about the way in which these guiding principles are applied in practice. There are fears that over-zealous corporate governance could undermine rather than strengthen company responses to security threats.

First, there is a danger that corporate governance methodologies applied in a security context will underline the misperception that all risks can be managed away. There is no such thing as absolute security, and some of the emerging security threats are causing serious headaches for policy-makers and decision-makers within companies who are struggling to find the most effective responses. This is at a time when there is greater pressure to find solutions, from a public panicked by pronouncements about the threat of terrorism of 'when, not if' from their political leaders. Substantive progress relies on being able to have open and frank discussions about the shortcomings of current approaches, and companies must look for frameworks that allow this type of exchange, both internally and with peers and competitors, without fear of undue criticism or reputational damage.

Security departments should avoid the temptation to exaggerate the extent to which they can deliver solutions. In the current climate, where many corporate security departments are enjoying unprecedented levels of interest from their senior management teams, it is especially important that they maintain a steady and modest line. Reinforcing the idea that security problems can be 'solved' will set up false expectations that will, ultimately, hinder a company's ability to make the necessary and difficult choices between competing priorities.

Second, and linked to this, the current climate of fear surrounding certain security risks makes it difficult to open up discussions about the law of diminishing returns relating to security spending. More money and effort does not necessarily bring greater security. It is important that companies do not feel compelled to 'look busy' while in practice their responses do little to tackle the threats. As one senior business executive noted, 'There is only so much we can do to prevent a determined agent. There is a grey area as far as expenditure is concerned between enforcing primitive security and creating Star Wars-like barriers. The jury is out on whether more expenditure equals more security or whether there is a law of diminishing returns.' These sorts of views rarely make it into public discourse.

Third, and perhaps most importantly, the foundation of effective security is trust, and there is a danger that over-formalised and rigid approaches to security undermine rather than reinforce trust. The most important trust relationship for a company in managing its security is with its own staff. There is growing appreciation that a company's best hope of protection comes from within: its staff constitute its most important intelligence network. Establishing strong relationships, which encourage and facilitate flows of information around a company, is key.

As well as being a source of information, staff are where security actually happens in practice. Security cannot be delivered discretely by a single department; it rests to a great extent on a company's ability to create a culture where employees understand their own role and responsibilities in delivering security. As one company representative commented, 'Rather than doubling the height of a fence around our plants, we have found that a far more valuable expenditure has been to make security increasingly a shared accountability for all our employees. Security is something we all play a part in enhancing, as opposed to it being something that is done to you by a small security team.' So-called 'commitment-based security' is explored in more detail in the chapter 'Hidden assets'.

## Beyond corporate governance

A recent report by the Institute for Business Ethics has documented a link between good corporate governance and good financial performance, but good corporate governance does not fully explain effective management.[19] For example, for many years Enron was held up as an exemplar of sound corporate governance; and, conversely, though Shell has been proved in hindsight to have been 'in the right' on the Brent Spa issue, being right was not enough to protect it in the face of opposition, and the events that followed caused it to change the way it does business. Having the correct structures in place does not seem to be enough.

### The way forward for companies

The jury is still out on whether or not corporate governance will make a substantial and positive contribution to the ability of companies to manage effectively the security challenges they face today. But it is clear that corporate governance as an organising principle for business decision-making is here to stay. Security professionals must step forward to play a leading role in shaping its impact on their day-to-day work and must initiate processes that seek answers to the outstanding questions and unpack the nature of the impact of corporate governance on security management.

Companies must also appreciate that it is impossible for them to operate in a vacuum. Their own attitudes and responses to security risks and their relationship to corporate governance must sit within a broader contextual understanding of wider and changing social attitudes to risk and the growing importance of reputation and perception. They must therefore position themselves as central players in the evolution of public debates about security, as well as those happening within their own organisations or even within the business community as a whole. This may open up potential reputational risks, but the risks of not coming to the decision-making table are likely to be much higher in the long term.

### Suggested further reading

The following books and articles expand on some of the arguments made in this report.

Adams, J, *Risk*. London: Routledge, 1995.
Hutter, B and Power, M, 'Risk management and business regulation',

CARR (Centre for Analysis of Risk and Regulation) launch paper, Oct 2000.

Power, M, *The Risk Management of Everything*. London: Demos, 2004.

Rayner, J, *Risky Business: Towards best practice in managing reputation risk*. Institute for Business Ethics, 2001.

*Risk and Regulation*, 4, Autumn 2002. Discussion between *Risk and Regulation* and CARR members Michael Power, Timothy Besley and Christopher Hood.

Webley, S, *Developing a Code of Business Ethics*. London: Institute for Business Ethics, 2003.

This report draws on discussions at a Demos seminar on 25 June 2004. Speakers at the seminar were **Philippa Foster-Back**, director of the Institute for Business Ethics; **Andrew Mackenzie**, group vice president for petrochemicals at BP; **Lucy Neville-Rolfe**, company secretary and director of corporate affairs at Tesco; and **John Smith**, head of group security at Prudential.

The seminar was part of a series supported by donations from a number of companies: Anite Public Sector, Astra Zeneca, BP, Control Risks Group, Group 4 Falck, HSBC, Kroll, Pfizer, Prudential and Shell.

# 5. Beyond measure
## Getting the maths of security right

### Overview

There is a growing appetite within corporate security departments and board rooms for greater 'quantification' within the security profession. Corporate security managers are keen to continue the professionalisation of security; they want better understanding of the threats and what works in managing them; and they are looking for ways to embed security into the everyday working practices and culture of their organisations.

Arguments rage about what types of information should be collected and how. And there are more complex debates beginning to surface about how information should be used and applied on a day-to-day level. This requires corporate security departments to consider factors such as the perceptions of employees, the decision-making processes of the board and senior management teams, and structural questions about where security should live within the company.

Ultimately, information is a means to an end – better and more confident judgement. Corporate security departments must maintain their focus on that objective, which is what their boards want from them and what reassures employees right across the company.

### The hunger for numbers

In recent years the 'quantification' of security has become a growing concern for corporate security departments and senior managers alike. There are five main reasons for this shift. First, corporate security managers have been keen to find ways to 'professionalise' their work; many are keen to gain a broader and deeper understanding of the threats facing their companies, the vulnerabilities in their corporate structures and cultures, and the most effective management responses. Second, and related, many believe that being able to measure some of these indicators will enhance the credibility of corporate security and give departments greater visibility and leverage within their organisations.

Third, those companies looking to implement a commitment-based security approach to security will need to be able to give employees information about the risks and what they can do each day to help to manage them. Fourth, the new complexity of security threats means that companies now tend to have a much shorter lead-in time to problems. This makes it even more critical that they are able to foresee problems and act swiftly to resolve them. The most obvious example of this is the threat from al Qaida and its related networks, which tends not to issue warnings before it attacks, but can be seen as a much broader trend, too. Fifth, and related to the last point, security has become an important and almost daily concern for employees, from the top of the organisation down. It is therefore not surprising that there is anecdotal evidence that boards and senior management teams are beginning to ask corporate security departments for the types of metrics and indicators they can expect from elsewhere in the company and that employees are initiating much more contact with the corporate security department.[20]

## What can be measured
There is considerable debate about the *types of information* that could be useful for corporate security departments, and the extent to which this can realistically be gathered.

The most straightforward thing to measure is *past incidents*. Companies regularly record information about breaches of security, from kidnapping and extortion to fraud and attacks on information technology systems. This approach tends to work well for high-frequency/low-impact crimes, where meaningful patterns can be observed. But it is less effective for predicting the likelihood of low-frequency/high-impact incidents, where it is usually difficult to obtain enough data to be statistically significant. Furthermore, the modus operandi of al Qaida has reminded corporate security professionals to expect the unexpected and that the past can often be more confusing than helpful in making sense of the future. It also tells the company nothing about whether it is effective *today* in tackling the threats it faces or about its adaptive capacity to respond to the future.

*Measuring the current or even future threats is only partially helpful* for companies making decisions about the way they manage security. For example, the threat of kidnapping in Colombia might be high, but if a company is operating in a part of the country where the threat is low it should not be an important consideration; if the threat of fraud in Nigeria is high but a company has only a very small office there, the likely impact overall will be low; and, conversely, though the threat of contamination in France is low, a food manufacturer whose main market is Europe and where the reputational impact of such an incident would be massive, will take even such a small threat very seriously. Companies must, therefore, combine information about threats with some form of assessment about their exposure and the likely impact on their operations. One simple way to understand this is to *measure risk (threat + exposure + impact) against materiality (assets, value – including reputation – and people).*

The ability of companies to manage security risks will not only depend on their own capabilities and vulnerabilities. They also rely on local *security forces or law enforcement agencies,* both in preventing particular incidents from occurring and more generally in helping to create conditions of stability rather than chaos. Some companies are beginning to try measuring this capability and are finding it an important variable. For example, while the threat of terrorism in the UK and US is high, the competence of the security forces means this presents a lower risk than that in Indonesia or Kenya, where the local forces are less able to prevent an attack.

This information can also *impact on the reach of the corporate security department.* In countries where the security forces are less competent, the reach of the security team grows; it is no longer just responsible for what happens within the place of work, but begins to assume responsibility for safety and security beyond the place of work, the perimeter of the facilities and even along transit routes, too.

## Perceptions of risk

Greater statistical data on security alone will not increase the credibility or visibility of corporate security. There is considerable evidence to show that an individual's *perceptions are driven by emotions rather than objective analysis* and this means that corporate security professionals will need much more than data tables to be convincing.

Paul Slovic's concept of the *'affect heuristic'* is helpful in understanding the relationship between decisions and information.[21] He argues that people make judgements about risk based on emotional calculation of costs and benefits. Affective judgements are holistic rather than analytic, focus on pleasure and pain rather than logic, and on free associations rather than on deductive connections. Slovic argues that they take the form of images, metaphors and narratives – all of which are deeply embedded in our therapeutic and democratic culture – rather than abstract symbols, words and numbers. They justify themselves – on the theory that 'experiencing is believing' – rather than requiring justification by logic and evidence. There is more detail on this in the chapter 'Perception gap'.

This analysis suggests that being 'right', and being able to prove it, is not enough; *corporate security departments must build effective narratives about the value of security within their companies, the nature of the threats they face and how management approaches fit within the broader business objectives and the daily routine of employees.* Maths is a useful tool, but it is no panacea.

## Applying the maths

The way that numbers are used by corporate security departments will vary greatly from company to company, according to culture and practices. Before they can make decisions about the practicalities of how information should be used and presented, there are more philosophical questions that corporate security departments must grapple with first.

### Approaches to maths in security

Professor Michael Power has identified two approaches to measurement and management in relation to operational risk: *calculative pragmatism* and *calculative idealism*.[22] Calculative pragmatism regards numbers as attention-directing strategies where risk-scoring systems make risk capital visible for management with the aim of steering behaviour in the right direction. This approach is commonly referred to as 'soft' risk management and suits environments where it is critical to identify and catalogue risks that lie at the limits of formal knowledge. Calculative idealism, on the other hand, regards numbers as representing the costs of true economic capital based on high quality frequency data, and suggesting correct economic behaviour in the light of these risk measures.

Although Power developed this distinction within the context of operational risk – particularly as it applies to Basel 2 – it raises important questions about the underlying rationale driving corporate security departments to seek out a more quantitative basis for their work.

### Practical lessons

It is a truism that information is only useful when it is used effectively. Having data is not enough; it needs to be operationalised and applied in the right way to work properly. In a study into manmade disasters, Turner and Pidgeon catalogue the factors that exacerbate the extent and scale of damage (see box below). There are a number of interesting observations: information is important, but it is one of many factors critical to effective management; information is only useful when its relevance is understood; and information can be destructive as well as instructive.

### Man-made disasters

Turner and Pidgeon carried out an in-depth analysis of three major man-made disasters: Aberfan, Hixon and the Summerland fire.[23] They reveal a pattern of events with the following similarities:

O *rigidities in perceptions and beliefs* in organisational settings, which prevented accurate perception of the possibility of the disaster

O the decoy problem: in a number of instances when some hazard was perceived, the action taken to deal with the problem distracted attention from the problem that eventually caused the disaster

O organisational exclusivity: disregard for non-members

O *information difficulties: a) completely unknown prior information, b) prior information noted but not fully appreciated, c) prior information noted by someone but not combined with other information at an appropriate time, d) prior information available but ignored because there was no place for it within prevailing modes of understanding*

O the involvement of strangers, especially on complex sites

O the minimising of emergent danger: a) an understanding of possible hazards, minimising emergent danger by insulating emotion against an idea which is accepted cognitively, b) *conflicting views about the danger*, c) changed awareness of the danger as attempts are made to control the situation, d) failure to call for help

O nature of recommendations after the disaster: the definition of well-structured problems; recommendations are designed to deal with the well-structured problem which has been defined and revealed by the disaster rather than with the ill-structured problem that existed before it.

## Security, maths and the board...

One of the most important drivers to develop more sophisticated types of information relating to security is to *enable the corporate security department to relate better to the board and senior management teams*. There is no doubt that boards have very specific information needs and the more corporate security departments are able to respond to these the better. But they must be mindful of the way that boards and senior management teams will use the information in practice.

## Relatives versus absolutes

Most senior managers do not have a working understanding of security, nor indeed most other business functions. Absolute numbers are therefore unlikely to be meaningful in helping them to make decisions. Instead, corporate security departments need to find ways to *illustrate trends over time*. This approach also helps senior managers to rate security alongside the full range of departmental requests, such as marketing, public affairs and sales.

## Judgement versus assessment

Boards want *judgement rather than assessment from their departmental leads because it makes it easier for them to make strategic decisions* about the future. Information about the past can, in many instances, offer clues about the future, but there are some areas of security where this is not the case. First, there are threats where the past is only instructive in reminding us to expect the unexpected next time. The most obvious example is the new breed of 'innovative' terrorism carried out by al Qaida and its associated networks. Second, there are threats where the past simply cannot tell us enough about the threat to help us to predict the future, such as is the case with low-frequency/high-impact threats. Third, changes in business practice and organisation over recent years and decades, from outsourcing and off-shoring to longer and more complicated supply chains, have made companies increasingly complex organisms. This complexity makes it much more difficult to predict the impact that an intervention will have. Ultimately, the future tends to be about intent; and that requires corporate security departments to make judgements rather than measurements.

## Timescales

*Boards and senior management teams tend to be working to shorter time horizons than corporate security departments* so there is a danger of presenting information that slips off their radar. This presents a dilemma for corporate security departments. Should they respond to this and focus on short-term priorities over the next one to two quarters and risk falling into a cycle of crisis response? Or should they push boards and senior managers to stretch their horizons to develop a more sustainable and less risky approach, but run the risk of diluting their own message? Corporate security departments must, of course, find a compromise between these two positions.

The rise of corporate governance has helped to lengthen the attention spans of boards so could be a useful framework for corporate security departments to work within. Layers of regulation require boards to adopt a longer-term view, and some of this now makes individual board members personally responsible. There is also growing speculation about the possible role for non-executive directors, who tend to have more time to devote to longer-term thinking.

## Structural influences

There is growing evidence to suggest that the position of corporate security within a company's structure has an important impact on the way security is managed and its ability to have an impact on corporate culture and working practices. For example, there is anecdotal evidence to suggest that it is useful for the corporate security department to associate itself with the audit and risk committees. It is always difficult to get business time, but integrating into the risk management structures can be one way of doing this. Of course, each company will have its own specific concerns and priorities, depending on its culture, history and values. The corporate security department must be sensitive to these factors and look for 'hooks' around which its work can be anchored.

## Lessons for companies

This report suggests a number of lessons for companies:

○ Companies must have a clear sense of why they want to gather information and data.
○ If companies are serious about using greater quantitative data, they must ensure they have the appropriate skills within their corporate security departments.
○ Companies must collect and collate data in a way that is most appropriate for its intended use.
○ Information must be stored in a way that allows it to be re-used at a later stage.
○ A clear distinction must be made between measurement, assessment and judgement.
○ Corporate security departments need to have a strategy for communicating with the rest of the company, and use different approaches for different people.
○ Presentation of data, trends and judgments is key: information must be presented in such a way that makes it easy for non-experts to spot trends over time.
○ Corporate security departments must ensure that the way they use and present the information is in keeping with their company's corporate culture.
○ Information must be related to the companies' business objectives.
○ Corporate security departments must be realistic about what can and cannot be measured: lack of hard data should not be a reason not to make a judgement.

## Suggested further reading

The following books and articles expand on some of the arguments made in this report.

Armor Group, *Securing the Knowledge Enterprise*, 2001.

Hausken, K, 'Probabalistic risk analysis and game theory', *Risk Analysis* 22, no 1, 2002, pp 17–27.

Kunreuther, H, 'Risk analysis and risk management in an uncertain world', paper for Distinguished Achievement Award for the Society for Risk Analysis Annual Meeting, Dec 2001 (also published in *Risk Analysis*).

Kunreuther, H, Novemsky, N and Kahneman, D, 'Making low probabilities useful', unpublished abstract paper, Dec 2000.

Power, M, 'The invention of operational risk', CARR Discussion Paper 16. London: London School of Economics, 2002.

Power, M, *The Risk Management of Everything*. London: Demos, 2004.

Rijpma, J, 'From deadlock to dead end: the normal accidents-high reliability debate revisited', *Journal of Contingencies and Crisis Management* 11, no 1, Mar 2003.

Rosen, J, *The Naked Crowd: Reclaiming security and freedom in an anxious age*. New York: Random House, 2004.

Simons, R, 'How risky is your company?' *Harvard Business Review* 77 no 3, May/June 1999, p85.

Turner, BA and Pidgeon, NF, *Man-made Disasters*, 2nd ed. Oxford: Butterworth-Heinemann, 1997.

Webley, S and More, E, *Does Business Ethics Pay? Ethics and financial performance*. London: Institute of Business Ethics, 2003.

'What is operational risk?' *Western Banking*, Jan 2002

Woo, G, 'Quantifying terrorism risk for insured portfolios', unpublished paper presented to the AON Conference, June 2003.

This report draws on discussions at a Demos seminar on 12 October 2004. Speakers at the seminar were **Robert Hall**, group assessments manager in the Group Financial Crime Department at Barclays; **Peter Cowap**, global compliance director at Diageo; and **Mike Basnett**, senior security adviser, and **James Husemeyer**, security analyst, from Shell.

The seminar was part of a series supported by donations from a number of companies: Anite Public Sector, Astra Zeneca, BP, Control Risks Group, Group 4 Falck, HSBC, Kroll, Pfizer, Prudential and Shell.

# 6. Invisible security

## The impact of counter-terrorism on the built environment

### Overview

Since the dawn of urbanisation, cities have provided rich pickings for bandits, petty criminals, protesters and terrorists, feeding off the city's economic, social and political wealth. To safeguard these treasures, urban and national rulers have peppered the cityscape with defensive features aimed at keeping undesirables out and controlling the movement of citizens within. From the city walls of ancient Rome to the checkpoints of modern-day Jerusalem and Belfast's so-called 'ring of steel', cities have been protected over the years by a range of physical and normally highly visible interventions.

In the aftermath of September 11, 2001, many architects, planners, politicians and academics worried that the new scale of threat posed by al Qaida and its associated networks would trigger an escalation of the 'militarisation' of our cities. Some argue they will become dominated by security, others that the threat of terrorism will leave them deserted and barren. One commentator has gone so far as to argue that the city will become the battleground of the twenty-first century: 'for the first time since the height of the Cold War issues surrounding international, military and geopolitical security now penetrate utterly into practices surrounding the governance, design and planning of cities and urban regions.'[24]

This paper tries to understand how the latest wave of counter-terrorism will impact on the built environment in the UK, with a special focus on British cities. The concerns that have been raised since September 11 have mostly come from across the Atlantic and feel familiar to built environment professionals who grappled with the challenge of Irish Republican terrorism on the mainland in the 1980s and 1990s. Britain's 30-year struggle against domestic terrorism puts it a generation ahead of the United States, whose first encounter with modern-day terrorism didn't come until 1995, when Timothy McVeigh blew up the Alfred P Murrah Federal Building in Oklahoma City, killing 168 people.

As Metropolitan Police commissioners, prime ministers and the Secretary-General of the Security Service continue to warn us that it is a case of 'when, not if' al Qaida manages to mount a successful terrorist attack in the UK, Britain is entering a new phase of counter-terrorism, which will re-write the principles of urban defence that have remained untouched for hundreds, even thousands, of years. Technological developments and design imperatives are turning counter-terrorism from a largely physical and visible activity (even when 'covert') into something which is almost invisible to the human eye. Planners will no longer have to rely on bulky security systems that restrict access and cause disruption to urban dwellers and terrorists alike. Instead, they will adopt light-touch security that, in the long term, will negate the need for the types of defences that are such a familiar feature on the urban landscape today.

'Invisible security' will change the relationship between counter-terrorism and the built environment. It will bring many benefits; it will make our cities look and feel better and could mark the beginning of the next urban renaissance. But invisible security also raises a number of challenges for urban governance: who makes decisions and how are they monitored, where does power lie, how will the use of these technologies differ between public and private spaces within cities, what is the balance between civil liberties and security within the context of the 'war on terror', and what role will built environment professionals find themselves playing?

Neither of these approaches – traditional urban defence and invisible security – grasps the 'human element' of counter-terrorism and the place of normal people in the governance and routines of our cities. In both, there is an assumption that security is something done 'to you' or 'for you', where the normal citizen is a passive spectator. Within the security world there is a growing recognition that truly effective security relies as much on getting widespread buy-in and active engagement, as on buying the right 'kit'. As clichéd as it might sound, normal people can become the 'eyes and ears' of the state, providing critical pieces of information for police and the security service by taking an active interest in their community. Security is delivered through small acts rather than grand gestures; normal people rather than clever scientists determine whether security systems work, depending on whether they stick to the rules or leave doors open and share passwords with colleagues. Ultimately, terrorism is a psychological game; terrorists feed not on the deaths of their victims, but on the fear and terror of those left behind. The resilience and resolve of ordinary citizens will dictate whether or not life in the city carries on as normal, and whether their perception of risk (rather than the reality of the risk of terrorism) will determine the nature of responses adopted in our cities.

The shift from traditional urban defence to invisible security offers exciting opportunities, but we must embrace the aesthetic possibilities without losing sight of the resulting challenges for effective urban governance. These debates must engage with a much wider range of individuals and organisations, and provide an interface between not just the people who design space and the people who secure space, but with those who use it, too. The long-term impact of counter-terrorism on the built environment will be measured in terms of the fabric of the city, but will be determined and framed by the nature of governance cultures and practices that exist at the city level. Getting the right answers to these questions will be key to preserving the vitality of our cities for generations to come.

## The relationship between counter-terrorism and the built environment

The relationship between counter-terrorism and the built environment in the UK can be understood within the context of the Irish Republican terrorist campaign that has spanned the last three decades. Over this period, there has been a gradual 'militarisation' of British cities – notably London and Belfast – which has made barricades, barriers, stop and search points and physical surveillance systems common features of the urban landscape. Although physical defences have been stepped up somewhat since September 11, there is no evidence to suggest this constitutes more than a gentle reinforcement of existing measures – an evolution rather than a revolution. While cities in the US – a country with little previous experience of domestic terrorism – consider radical proposals for security, British cities are merely consolidating what they already have in place.

The impact of counter-terrorism on the built environment relates as much to the psychological as the physical. As Ellin has argued, 'form follows fear' on the urban landscape.[25] In the wake of the anthrax attacks in the US in autumn 2001, for example, companies in London reported installing beefed-up security measures in their offices not because they believed there was a heightened threat, but to calm the fears of their employees.[26] This kind of response is understandable; in opinion polls on both sides of the Atlantic, the public consistently cites terrorism, foreign policy and defence as being among their most important concerns.[27]

In the so-called 'war on terror', cities are not just functional spaces that provide physical defence from attack. The cityscape is an important canvas for our hopes and fears. There is an intimate relationship between the look and feel of a city and the way people within the space feel about themselves and one another. The future shape of urban landscapes, therefore will help to determine whether we win the psychological battle in the war on terrorism. The point at which iconic buildings and ambitious designs seem dangerous decisions is precisely the moment we need to embrace them more enthusiastically than ever before. Evidence from the street provides cause for optimism.

Broadly speaking, there are three main ways in which counter-terrorism impacts in a physical way on the built environment: the militarisation of space through the use of physical security barriers; the demise of iconography in the urban landscape – in other words what we choose *not* to build; and a process of decentralisation as companies and ordinary people decide the risks of terrorism outweigh the benefits of city life.

## The 'militarisation' of urban space

Belfast is one of the best examples of the impact of counter-terrorism on the built environment. In his book on the subject, Jon Coaffee describes the use of 'fortress architecture' and 'defensible space' in the city, 'notably around the central shopping area in Belfast where access to the centre was barred, first by concrete blockers and barbed wire, and then later by a series of high metal gates which became known as the "ring of steel" – a term which was to gain new meaning in the 1990s in central London'. He describes how these design principles had a profound impact on the look of the city, the way residents and visitors used the space, and how they felt about being there.[28]

When the Irish Republican terrorist campaign reached the mainland, London drew heavily on this experience, though the outcome was less severe. There was no overarching strategy, but rather a number of measures were adopted in response to attacks or intelligence about intended or probable targets. For example, in 1989 wrought-iron gates were erected at the end of Downing Street to restrict access to authorised visitors; and in July 1993 London got its own 'ring of steel', which reduced from 30 to seven the number of entrances to the City, with each road-block watched by armed police. Around this time, closed circuit television (CCTV) was also being rolled out across the capital. In the intervening years, particularly since September 11, London has updated its security measures, notably around the US embassy and the Houses of Parliament.

Although London and a handful of other cities adopted physical security measures to guard against the terrorist threat, smaller and medium-sized cities have done much less. On the one hand, this should not worry us because intelligence suggests that London remains by far the most important and likely target. On the other hand, the new Civil Contingencies Bill devolves responsibility for contingencies planning and response to the local level. Faced with this legislation and the fears of local residents and businesses, local authorities may be forced to pick up their pace.

The militarisation of urban space is not always an effective tool in the fight against terrorism. First, the costs of security must be balanced against the benefits. In the immediate aftermath of September 11, hysteria raised public security spending in the United States to a level that no country could possibly sustain. The US Attorney General estimated that the government's response to the 2001 anthrax attacks cost $5 billion, and some federal offices remain closed more than three years later.

Second, security is not a risk-free strategy. Following the bombing of its consulate in Istanbul in 2003, the British Foreign and Commonwealth Office (FCO) undertook a review of security arrangements at its posts around the world to work out whether security needed to be increased. In his report to Parliament in June 2004, Jack Straw acknowledged that the FCO's buildings and staff are at risk in a number of key locations, especially where the UK is seen as being a 'softer' target than the US. But he rejected a 'fortress' response because of the detrimental effect it would have on its operational effectiveness and its relationship with local communities on the ground. The FCO made a calculated assessment that in most parts of the world the risks of isolation outweigh the risks from terrorism.[29]

Third, highly visible security not only sends the message 'we take security seriously'; it also says, 'we *need* to take security seriously', which can be less reassuring. The British government's handling of the 2001 outbreak of foot and mouth disease provides a useful example of how such perceptions can have disastrous and unintended consequences. Keen to show his electorate he was taking the crisis seriously, Prime Minister Blair took measures to show he was leading the response from the front. Part of this involved him visiting affected areas wearing the mandatory protective suit. While this played well at home, pictures of Tony Blair in a 'moon suit' gave the impression to those outside the country that Britain was closed for business, and wiped £2 billion off tourism revenues that year. As Alastair Campbell, director of communications at Downing Street at the time reflected, 'you get these dramatic pictures of the Prime Minister wearing yellow suits and walking around a farmyard, and in America they think "Christ! He's got to wear a yellow suit! And he's the Prime Minister."'[30]

### The end of urban iconography

Al Qaida is a terrorist network that is aware of the power of symbols and the symbols of power. On the morning of September 11, 2001, its lieutenants turned four aeroplanes – physical symbols of globalisation and progress – into weapons and flew them into the World Trade Center, the symbol of global trade, and the Pentagon, home of US military might. It is thought the fourth plane was heading towards the White House.

As a result of this, many have argued that planners and architects – led by their clients – will turn their backs on iconography in favour of uniformity. Peter Marcuse has predicted that obtrusive skyscrapers will lose some of their appeal. He observes the impact of the September 11 attacks on the Empire State Building: 'A consultant working on the 44th floor is quoted as saying he's considering buying a parachute and found one on the internet for $130. Five months after September 11th, a business newspaper headlines on its front page: "Empire State emptying out as tenants flee. Anxiety lingers; vacant space triples." Marcuse has a vision of more sober-looking cities: 'less high-rise, less representative, less "signature" fashion' developments in the future.[31]

There is little evidence to suggest that our urban landscapes will shrink or become less interesting: the re-development of the site of the World Trade Center will contain a building even taller than the twin towers; and, in London, the Greater London Authority continues to encourage tall buildings at the heart of London's two financial districts,[32] and a 2002 report from the Transport, Local Government and the Regions Select Committee of the House of Commons promotes the benefits of well-designed tall buildings.[33] There is also a plethora of high-rises currently in construction that will rival anything that has gone before them. Rem Koolhaas has designed an 80-storey tower in Beijing for China Central Television; the Shanghai World Financial Centre will dwarf Kuala Lumpar's Twin Petronas Towers as the world's tallest building; and another eight of the world's tallest buildings are currently under construction in the Far East.[34]

This is partially explained by economics: real-estate prices in global cities such as New York and London create a strong incentive to build up rather than out. The explanation is also cultural and psychological, though. The urban landscape has come to reflect and project how we feel about ourselves and what we want to become. Bold architecture has become a weapon for the competitive multinational seeking to stand out in a crowded marketplace; city planners understand the pulling power of creative architecture; and, in the face of terrorism, urban growth and renewal help a society to face up to its fears and win the psychological battle of wills. Clausewitz, the famous Prussian military thinker and strategist, argued that you only win when your opponent backs down, and modern-day commentators such as James Woudhuysen have cautioned architects and planners about the danger of answering public fears with less ambitious and more cautious constructions.[35] The urban landscape provides a means through which ordinary people can communicate that the fight continues.

## Decentralisation

A number of urban commentators have argued that the threat from al Qaida may challenge the future of our cities, as more and more people and organisations move out of urban areas. Three and a half years on from September 11, there is no evidence to suggest that the lure of New York is any weaker. One-third of Class A real estate in downtown New York was lost as a result of the September 11 attacks, but within a matter of weeks most companies had managed to find alternative spaces within the downtown area or were facing temporary displacements in the meantime.[36]

This echoes London's experience. The 'pull' of the city usually remains greater than the 'push' from terrorism. During the Irish Republican terror campaign in London in the 1980s and 1990s, very few companies relocated out of the city. In a recent poll of business in London, while 40 per cent of respondents said terrorism was the most important risk facing the capital, only 3 per cent said it was a factor that would influence whether or not they would relocate out of London.[37] The most important factors were business rates and insurance. In fact, the threat of decentralisation only surfaced in London when insurance premiums against terrorism rose sharply in the early 1990s. The creation of the PoolRe insurance scheme around that time proved extremely successful and removed insurance as a factor affecting location.[38] This scheme has recently been updated to reflect changes in the nature of the threat since September 11.

Perhaps the most striking example of the lure of urban proximity is Jerusalem, one of the cities most badly ravaged by terrorism and violence in recent years. In comparison with Tel Aviv, security risks are much higher in Jerusalem, but there is no evidence to suggest this had had a detrimental impact on the city's growth and development. In the 50 years since Israel became a state, Jerusalem's share of the total population of Israel has grown and its average annual population growth has been a healthy 4.2 per cent, as opposed to 2.6 per cent in Tel Aviv. Jerusalem's physical beauty, strong tourist economy and historical significance for both the country and the region as a whole outweigh the relative dangers of terrorism.[39]

The big unknown is the impact that a biological or chemical attack would have on the built environment. In the short term, experts are largely agreed that it will be several years before there is a credible risk that al Qaida or its associated networks will be capable of launching such an attack. Most of the substances they are developing are relatively easy to produce, but difficult to do so in an operational format that would bring death and destruction on anything but a very local scale. This was evident in the Sarin gas attack on the Tokyo subway by the terrorist cult group Aum Shinrikyo in 1995, which caused large-scale panic but killed only 12 people. The psychological impact of even a small-scale attack at a tube station or on a packed commuter train could be significant, and might be the trigger that prompts individuals to ask whether they really need to live and work in one of the world's most important terrorist targets.

## The rise of 'invisible security'

While barricades and barriers defined the counter-terrorist urban landscape of the 1990s in the UK, in recent years there have been significant attempts to 'tone down' security in cities. This trend looks set to accelerate in the coming years, aided by developments in technology that negate the need for bulky and obtrusive security, and as planners and architects begin to think more creatively about how they can hide security behind design features. As a result, security is becoming 'invisible' to the naked eye. While this might make our cities look and feel nicer to spend time in, and reduce the inconveniences associated with security, it raises critical questions about the governance of cities, which architects, designers and planners need to engage with as a matter of priority.

### Sensitive security

Over recent years, attempts to counter-balance security features with aesthetically pleasing design have coincided with an urban renaissance that has been transforming our cities for the last five to ten years. In some cases, this might be limited to small touches that make a subtle, but important, difference to the way a building, road or area looks. For example, the concrete barriers erected outside the Houses of Parliament following the September 11 attacks have recently been painted black to make them less obtrusive; and other barriers have been replaced by sturdy but more attractive flowering plant pots.[40]

In other cases, security has been factored into the design process from the outset. For example, instead of using a conventional barrier, designers of a pedestrian path that will link the ferry terminal on the Hudson River to the site of the World Trade Center designed a luminous glass bench. It will provide seating, subtly glowing illumination and aesthetic delight, while performing the important role of keeping vehicle threats at bay. It will be lower than a typical barrier because in front of the bench there will be compressible fill material that will support people but cause vehicles to sink down.[41] These types of clever designs are likely to become more common in the future.

### Next generation counter-terrorism technologies

Developments in technology will make security less visible, but much more invasive in the future. In particular, as biometric technologies come of age they will radically alter the principles underpinning the governance of security at the street level, by changing the relationship between the observer and the observed, and making decision-making much less visible.

There are numerous examples of the development and implementation of such technologies. In Schiphol airport in the Netherlands, an airport-wide system of iris recognition technology is being deployed for users of the airport. At the moment the scheme is voluntary – in fact, you have to pay $100 to take part – but if it proves successful it will become mandatory. Not only will it aid security at the airport, but it is hoped it will eventually do away with the need for credit cards in airport shops.[42] Security officials will be able to run checks against those using the airport and cross-reference with lists of known criminals or terrorists. A similar technology is already in use in many shops across the UK to tackle shoplifting.

In July 2003, it was reported that the Pentagon was developing a digitalised surveillance network that is capable of tracking the movements of all vehicles in a city by identifying them by physical characteristic, colour or even the biometric features of the driver. This expansive 'tracking system' has already attracted the attention of the law enforcement agencies keen to mainstream this military technology for non-combat use.[43]

London's 'ring of steel' has been superseded in recent years by what might be termed a 'ring of glass'. It is estimated that drivers in London are caught on camera three times during an average journey through the city.[44] Not only do the hundreds of CCTV cameras in London catch drivers entering the congestion zone without paying, they also provide an invaluable surveillance network for the police and security service. In fact, MI5, Special Branch and the Metropolitan Police are reported to have helped to develop software installed on the cameras, which automatically identifies suspects or known criminals who enter the eight-square-mile zone. There are currently more than 30 cities across the UK that are watching London carefully, waiting to replicate the congestion scheme if it proves successful. The nationwide roll-out of the scheme would be relatively rapid because the UK has the most comprehensive CCTV network of any country, with 2.5 million CCTV cameras, or 10 per cent of the world's total.

These developments could bring enormous benefits. First, if they deliver results, they could become a critical part of crime and terrorism prevention strategies across the country. Those known to the authorities could be singled out, monitored and if necessary taken in for questioning. Second, because these technologies are less invasive it could remove many of the inconveniences we all face in the name of security – the checkpoint, the diversion, the no-entry sign, and so on. In short, they allow 'normal' life to go on; they create what planners call 'permeable' cities, but provide the means to eradicate certain types of behaviour. Third, it might change the way our cities look and feel. Reducing the need for invasive and clunky security allows local authorities, planners and designers to concentrate on the aesthetics of the city, using design to create the types of spaces that are inclusive and welcoming.

We should caution against the unfettered adoption of such technologies, though. There are of course concerns about the impact on civil liberties. This debate is well rehearsed in its traditional form. But within this context it is particularly important to note that the erosion of civil liberties unpicks the democratic contract between citizens and politicians that is essential in the delivery of counter-terrorism. If normal citizens are to act as 'unlikely counter-terrorists', there must be a relationship of trust and mutual engagement on which to base this.[45]

Wherever there is technology, there is the perennial danger of 'function creep', which makes governance opaque. As Gareth Crossman of the campaign group Liberty has said:

> *There is an issue we are concerned about which is called 'function creep'. This is where we are told that a system is being set up and used for a certain purpose and then we find out it is being used for another totally different one. It is a dangerous precedent. We would be concerned that it would be just a 'fishing' exercise where large amounts of data are passed over to the police or the security services and they just sift through it.*

Who decides what type of behaviour is 'unacceptable' and in need of monitoring? Is there any power of veto over inappropriate uses of this technology in *private* space? How do we keep track of what this technology is being used for, especially function creep into other areas outside the agreed remit?

There is always a danger that policy-makers put too much faith into technologies to deliver where non-technological means have failed. The rapid deployment of CCTV provides a good example. Throughout the 1980s and 1990s, the growing risk posed by frequent and severe terrorist attacks on the mainland by the IRA and the growing fear of crime among the public caught policy-makers and politicians off guard. The growing visibility of persistent poverty and degradation in many inner city areas, an alcohol-fuelled 'yob culture', a drugs-induced crime wave and the rise of sensational media reporting of these and other issues such as child abduction, paedophilia and violent crime left many people fearing that Britain was in the middle of a crime epidemic.

Around this time, CCTV was already beginning to be used on private property, such as in shops. The hope was that it could also help to tackle problems in public spaces, too. There was no evidence of the effectiveness of CCTV in crime prevention, but a massive programme of CCTV development started, regardless. Initiated by the last Conservative government, it was keenly continued by Labour when it came into office in 1997. John Major devoted more than three-quarters of the crime prevention budget to encourage local authorities to install CCTV and between 1996 and 1998 CCTV became the single most heavily funded non-criminal justice crime prevention measure. What started on a small scale in London to protect against terrorist attacks quickly spread out to the rest of the country. It is now estimated that the average Briton is photographed by more than 300 separate cameras from 30 separate CCTV networks in one day.[46]

This investment was made without any evidence about the effectiveness of CCTV in either preventing crime or increasing the level of detection and successful prosecution. It seemed sensible to assume that if people knew they were being watched they would be less likely to commit crime. However, a recent study commissioned by the Home Office has found that CCTV has not brought any measurable decrease in terrorism or crime, partly because criminals quickly learn to adapt their behaviour and partly because the success of technology is determined more by the social context within which it is used and the ability of its operatives than by the hardware itself.[47]

Research and polling continues to show that CCTV makes the public *feel* safer, and pressure mounts for further expansion of coverage. This reminds us of Ellin's warning that 'form follows fear' and begs the question of whether built environment professionals, policy-makers and politicians should meet real or perceived risks.

As physical security retreats and becomes less visible there are likely to be psychological effects. People might begin to feel less safe as the symbols of security disappear, concerned that nothing seems to be happening. There is also a danger that as security retreats ordinary people lose the sense of their own role in the security matrix. Security is not something that can be done 'to you'; it requires individuals to adopt an active rather than a passive demeanour. It is important that technological developments do not leave individuals disempowered; not only would this break their spirit but would also result in less effective outcomes.

Also at stake is a fundamental question about how the development of invisible security will change the nature of the urban space. Peter Marcuse has argued that 'security [has] become[s] the justification for measures that threaten the core of urban social and political life, from the physical barricading of space to the social barricading of democratic activity'. He argues that rising levels of security in cities will reduce the public use of public space and the levels of popular participation in governmental planning and the decision-making process by making public protest more difficult and making individuals feel alienated in public places.[48] At a time when these security measures themselves make governance more rather than less important, this is an alarming prediction.

Cities have traditionally been anonymous places where creativity and eccentricity meet to produce works of art, music, thinking and writing. It remains to be seen whether this chemistry can be maintained alongside heightened monitoring and surveillance, although Orwell's *1984* – with his all-seeing telescreen – offers a disturbing vision of what this kind of future might look like.[49] The impact would not just be cultural and social; the death of bohemianism in our cities would have an economic impact, too. Richard Florida has argued that it is the cities that are able to capture a 'creative class', which prosper most, and has shown evidence from the US and Europe to sustain his thesis.[50]

## Community-based counter-terrorism – the potential of sustainable communities

Both traditional urban defence and invisible security rely heavily on the idea that security is 'delivered' and fundamentally fail to recognise the role of individuals and communities in contributing towards counter-terrorism from the bottom up. At a time when al Qaida is trying to establish a home-grown network in the UK, through secondary and sometimes even tertiary networks, it is more important than ever before that counter-terrorism is a locally based, community level activity, as well as something which is driven by strategic policy priorities from the very top of government. It is only by working at this level that we will be able to starve the network's oxygen and prevent it from establishing a domestic base from which to launch attacks within the UK much more easily.[51]

The concept of 'sustainable communities' seems to offer an alternative approach to counter-terrorism, which would focus on the interface between the built environment, people and security, based on an understanding of how people use space in practice. Inspired by 'crime prevention through environmental design' (CPTED),[52] sustainable communities are now at the heart of UK planning policy. They are described in a recent paper for the Office of the Deputy Prime Minister (ODPM) as 'communities which succeed now, economically, socially and environmentally, and respect the needs of future generations. They are well designed places where people feel safe and secure; where crime and disorder, or the fear of crime, doesn't undermine quality of life or community cohesion.'[53] This is reinforced by the new Planning Policy Statement 1, which has put crime prevention at the heart of the planning process: 'Designing out crime and designing in community safety should be central to the planning and delivery of new development.'[54]

Sustainable communities are organised around seven attributes, some of which are relevant to counter-terrorism:

O   access and movement: places with well-defined routes, spaces and entrances that provide for convenient movement without compromising security; this makes it easier to spot unusual behaviour within these spaces

O   structure: places that are structured so that different users do not cause conflict

O   surveillance: places where all publicly accessible spaces are overlooked; this is a human alternative to CCTV coverage and puts people rather than machines at the centre of surveillance efforts

O   ownership: places that promote a sense of ownership, respect, territorial responsibility and community and therefore encourage people to be proactive rather than passive in the security of their spaces

O    physical protection: places that include necessary, well-designed security features, but which allow normal life to continue

O    activity: places where the level of human activity is appropriate to the location and creates a reduced risk of crime and a sense of safety at all times

O    management and maintenance: places that are designed with management and maintenance in mind, to discourage crime in the present and the future.

The concept of sustainable communities is currently focused on the potential for built form and design features to tackle crime, and the results seem to be encouraging. There is as yet no precedent within the 'war on terror' to adopt a similar approach to counter-terrorism, but it is an interesting idea and the built environment community should explore further whether this type of approach to urban planning and design would make terrorism more difficult while maintaining many of the positive attributes of the city.

Just as CPTED and sustainable communities sprang partly from a frustration with the negative impacts resulting from more traditional approaches to crime prevention, so we could well find ourselves on the cusp of a new sense of dissatisfaction with the way we are handling terrorism, which promises to unpick all the good work we did in the 1990s. As David Dixon, principal in charge of planning and urban design at Goody, Clancy and Associates in Boston, puts it:

*It is perhaps the greatest irony that in recent decades much of our urban environment was rescued from fear – and cities and societies were made far safer – by the conscious creation of more open buildings, the blurring of the separation of public and private space, the promotion of community, and the drawing of people back to our streets and squares. A single-minded focus on defending against terrorism threatens all of these hard-won gains.*[55]

## Conclusion

Cities have been the site of war, crime, disorder, riots and terrorism since the dawn of urbanisation. City walls may have made way for 'rings of steel', but the principles of urban defence have largely remained the same for centuries.

These principles are beginning to be challenged by the rise of 'invisible security', which is seeing security shift from being a physical and visible function to something that is largely unseen by the human eye. Invisible security is facilitated by new technological developments, such as biometrics, and has been encouraged by fans of good urban design who argue that obtrusive security robs a city of its soul. Indeed, invisible security offers exciting opportunities for urban development.

It also raises many important questions about the way our cities are managed and governed: who makes decisions, where power lies, and how technology is being used behind the scenes. This is not necessarily an impossible course to navigate, but given the pace of technological change and the climate of fear present across the UK at the moment, it is important that we grapple with this and explore ways in which we can use invisible security to further the process of opening up cities, making them more permeable and more inclusive for a wider range of people, while at the same time asking difficult questions about urban governance.

This paper has argued strongly that security is not delivered 'to you' or 'for you', but relies on the active engagement of normal people, too. Security is delivered through small acts as well as grand gestures and the choices we make as a society about risk and response can ultimately be traced back to a set of personal and social psychological processes. This human factor is strikingly absent from the two security models set out, traditional urban defence and invisible security, where the individual plays a largely passive role.

Achieving a positive relationship between counter-terrorism and the built environment will rest on our ability to find ways of bringing together those who design spaces with those who secure it and those who use it to explore new urban forms which can deliver people-centred counter-terrorism, perhaps using the sustainable communities model as a starting point. But securing our cities is more than a technical process. We also need to create new cultures of engagement that spawn the types of urban governance needed for people-centred counter-terrorism to work in practice. Sustainable communities provide a good example of how the built environment can – by design – *enable* individuals to play an active role. It could be said that the design itself helps to facilitate the creation and re-creation of new types of urban governance.

Our cities have come to hold a special role, acting as everything from centres of creativity and economic might to the canvas for the national psyche. At a time when there is a growing understanding of the role to be played in counter-terrorism by individuals and communities, we must ensure we move beyond just technical and mechanical responses to terrorism. Securing the future of cities will require us to reinvigorate a much wider debate about the types of democratic cultures that can keep our cities vibrant and safe for generations to come.

## Suggested further reading

Demkin, JA (ed), *Security Planning and Design: A guide for architects and building design professionals.* Hoboken, NJ: Wiley, 2004.

Kotkin, J and Siegel, F, 'Terrorism: attacks threaten the future of cities', *Los Angeles Times*, 14 Oct 2001.

Nadel, BA (ed), *Building Security: Handbook for architectural planning and design.* New York; London: McGraw-Hill, 2004.

Newman, O, *Creating Defensible Space.* Washington DC: US Dept of Housing and Urban Development, Office of Policy Development and Research, 1996.

Pawley, M, *Terminal Architecture.* London: Reaktion, 1998.

Russell, J, *Designing for Security: Using art and design to improve security.* New York: Art Commission of the City of New York and Design Trust for Public Space, 2002.

Vergano, D, 'Experts seek safety in future buildings', *USA Today*, 17 Sep 2001.

Warren, R, 'Situating the city and September 11th: military urban doctrine, "pop-up" armies and spatial chess', *International Journal of Urban and Regional Research* 26 no 3, Sep 2002, pp 614–19.

This paper was commissioned by the Commission for Architecture and the Built Environment (CABE) and presented at a CABE seminar in March 2005. It is published by Demos in cooperation with CABE under the terms of Demos' open access publishing licence.

# Notes

1 G Mulgan, *Network Logic* (London: Demos, 2004).
2 C Donnelly, Demos Annual Security Lecture, Dec 2004.
3 R Cooper, *The Post Modern State and the World Order* (London: Demos, 2000).
4 See: http://news.bbc.co.uk/1/hi/technology/4413155.stm (accessed 26 May 2005).
5 See: http://news.bbc.co.uk/1/hi/uk/3687628.stm (accessed 26 May 2005).
6 See: www.publications.parliament.uk/pa/cm200405/cmselect/cmhaff/165/16502.htm (accessed 26 May 2005).
7 Sir David Veness, 'The Unlikely Counter-Terrorists', lecture for Demos, 22 Feb 2005. For more information, see www.demos.co.uk.
8 Quoted in J Rosen, *The Naked Crowd: Reclaiming security and freedom in an anxious age* (New York: Random House, 2004).
9 Donnelly, Demos Annual Security Lecture.
10 J Flynn, P Slovic and H Kunreuther (eds), *Risk, Media and Stigma: Understanding public challenges to modern science and technology* (London: Earthscan, 2001).
11 G le Bon, *The Crowd: A study of the popular mind* (Mineola NY: Dover Publications, 2002).
12 A Tversky and D Kahnemann, 'Availability: a heuristic for judging frequency and probability', *Cognitive Psychology* 5 (1973).
13 G Gerbner, 'Violence and terror in and by the media' in M Raboy and B Dagenais (eds), *Media, Crisis and Democracy* (London: Sage, 1992).
14 Quoted in Rosen, *The Naked Crowd*.
15 W Kip Viscusi, 'Alarmist decisions with divergent risk information', *Economic Journal* 107 (1997).
16 RF Knight and DJ Pretty, *Reputation and Value: The case of corporate catastrophes* (Oxford: Metrica, 2001).
17 Janusian Security Risk Management, 'Behind the lines: terrorism risk and the private sector', unpublished conference report, 2003.
18 For a more detailed discussion of 'adaptive capacities', please see J Chapman,

*System Failure: Why governments must learn to think differently* (London: Demos, 2004) and T Bentley and J Wilsdon (eds) *The Adaptive State: Strategies for personalising the public realm* (London: Demos, 2003), both available to download free of charge from www.demos.co.uk.

19    S Webley, *Developing a Code of Business Ethics* (London: Institute for Business Ethics, 2003).

20    For case study information see R Briggs, *Doing Business in a Dangerous World* (London: Foreign Policy Centre, 2003). This report is available to download free of charge at www.fpc.org.uk.

21    Flynn, Slovic and Kunreuther, *Risk, Media and Stigma*.

22    M Power, 'The invention of operational risk', CARR Discussion Paper 16, 2002.

23    BA Turner and NF Pidgeon, *Man-made Disasters*, 2nd ed (Oxford: Butterworth-Heinemann, 1997).

24    S Graham, 'Special collection: reflections on cities, September 11th and the "War on Terror" – one year on', *International Journal of Urban and Regional Research* 26 no 3 (2002).

25    N Ellin, 1997, cited in J Coaffee, *Terrorism, Risk and the City: The making of a contemporary urban landscape* (Aldershot: Ashgate, 2003).

26    Based on off-the-record research interviews with the security directors of six major multinationals based in London, conducted as part of the research project for Briggs, *Doing Business in a Dangerous World.*

27    March 2004 poll: www.mori.com/polls/2004/mpm040316.shtml (accessed 26 May 2005).

28    Coaffee, *Terrorism, Risk and the City.*

29    'Review of FCO security overseas', written ministerial statement, 29 June 2004.

30    Quoted in M Leonard with C Stead and C Smewing, *Public Diplomacy* (London: Foreign Policy Centre, 2002).

31    P Marcuse, 'Urban form and globalisation after September 11th: the view from New York', *International Journal of Urban and Regional Research*, 26 no 3 (Sep 2002).

32    Coaffee, *Terrorism, Risk and the City.*

33    *Tall Buildings*, Sixteenth Report of Session 2001–02, Vol 1, House of Commons Transport, Local Government and the Regions Committee, www.parliament.the-stationery-office.co.uk/pa/cm200102/cmselect/cmtlgr/482/482.pdf (accessed 26 May 2005).

34    J Woudhuysen and I Abley, *Why is Construction so Backward?* (Chichester: Wiley-Academy, 2004).

35    Ibid.

36    E Glaeser and J Shapiro, *Cities and Warfare: The impact of terrorism on urban form* (Cambridge MA: Harvard Institute of Economic Research, Dec 2001).

37    June 2003 poll: www.mori.com/polls/2003/cima-top.shtml (accessed 26 May 2005).

38    Coaffee, *Terrorism, Risk and the City*

39    Glaeser and Shapiro, *Cities and Warfare.*

40    Coaffee, *Terrorism, Risk and the City.*

41    P Langdon, 'Three years after 9/11, security mindset threatens civic design', *New Urban News* (Sep 2004).

42    M Mills and P Huber, 'How technology will defeat terrorism', *City Journal* (Winter 2002).

43    J Coaffee, 'Rings of steel, rings of concrete and rings of confidence: designing out terrorism in central London pre and post September 11th', *International Journal of Urban and Regional Research* 28, no 1 (Mar 2004).

44    M Townsend and P Harris, 'Security role for traffic cameras', *Observer*, 9 Feb 2003.

45    The concept of the 'unlikely counter-terrorists' was developed in a collection edited by Rachel Briggs in 2002: *The Unlikely Counter-Terrorists* (London: Foreign Policy Centre, 2002).

46    Rosen, *The Naked Crowd.*

47    BC Welsh and DP Farringdon, *Crime Prevention Effects of Closed Circuit Television: A systematic review*, Home Office Research Study 252 (London: Home Office, 2002).

48    Marcuse, 'Urban form and globalisation after September 11th'.

49    G Orwell, *1984* (Harmondsworth: Penguin, 1949).

50    R Florida, *The Rise of the Creative Class: and how it's transforming work, leisure, community and everyday life* (New York: Basic Books, 2002).

51    This is a point made by Sir David Veness, outgoing Assisstant Commissioner for Specialist Operations at the Metropolitan Police at a recent lecture for Demos, *The Unlikely Counter-Terrorists*, 22 Feb 2005. For more information, see www.demos.co.uk.

52    CPTED is based on the assumption that crime can be designed out of a space if it is a consideration from the outset of development.

53    ODPM, *Safer Places: The planning system and crime prevention* (London: Office of the Deputy Prime Minister, 2004).

54    ODPM, *Delivering Sustainable Development*, Planning Policy Statement 1 (London: Office of the Deputy Prime Minister, 2005).

55    P Langdon, 'Three years after 9/11, security mindset threatens civic design'.

# DEMOS – Licence to Publish

1.  **Definitions**
    a   **"Collective Work"** means a work, such as a periodical issue, anthology or encyclopedia, in which the Work in its entirety in unmodified form, along with a number of other contributions, constituting separate and independent works in themselves, are assembled into a collective whole. A work that constitutes a Collective Work will not be considered a Derivative Work (as defined below) for the purposes of this Licence.
    b   **"Derivative Work"** means a work based upon the Work or upon the Work and other pre-existing works, such as a musical arrangement, dramatization, fictionalization, motion picture version, sound recording, art reproduction, abridgment, condensation, or any other form in which the Work may be recast, transformed, or adapted, except that a work that constitutes a Collective Work or a translation from English into another language will not be considered a Derivative Work for the purpose of this Licence.
    c   **"Licensor"** means the individual or entity that offers the Work under the terms of this Licence.
    d   **"Original Author"** means the individual or entity who created the Work.
    e   **"Work"** means the copyrightable work of authorship offered under the terms of this Licence.
    f   **"You"** means an individual or entity exercising rights under this Licence who has not previously violated the terms of this Licence with respect to the Work, or who has received express permission from DEMOS to exercise rights under this Licence despite a previous violation.
2.  **Fair Use Rights.** Nothing in this licence is intended to reduce, limit, or restrict any rights arising from fair use, first sale or other limitations on the exclusive rights of the copyright owner under copyright law or other applicable laws.
3.  **Licence Grant.** Subject to the terms and conditions of this Licence, Licensor hereby grants You a worldwide, royalty-free, non-exclusive, perpetual (for the duration of the applicable copyright) licence to exercise the rights in the Work as stated below:
    a   to reproduce the Work, to incorporate the Work into one or more Collective Works, and to reproduce the Work as incorporated in the Collective Works;
    b   to distribute copies or phonorecords of, display publicly, perform publicly, and perform publicly by means of a digital audio transmission the Work including as incorporated in Collective Works;
    The above rights may be exercised in all media and formats whether now known or hereafter devised. The above rights include the right to make such modifications as are technically necessary to exercise the rights in other media and formats. All rights not expressly granted by Licensor are hereby reserved.
4.  **Restrictions.** The licence granted in Section 3 above is expressly made subject to and limited by the following restrictions:
    a   You may distribute, publicly display, publicly perform, or publicly digitally perform the Work only under the terms of this Licence, and You must include a copy of, or the Uniform Resource Identifier for, this Licence with every copy or phonorecord of the Work You distribute, publicly display, publicly perform, or publicly digitally perform. You may not offer or impose any terms on the Work that alter or restrict the terms of this Licence or the recipients' exercise of the rights granted hereunder. You may not sublicense the Work. You must keep intact all notices that refer to this Licence and to the disclaimer of warranties. You may not distribute, publicly display, publicly perform, or publicly digitally perform the Work with any technological measures that control access or use of the Work in a manner inconsistent with the terms of this Licence Agreement. The above applies to the Work as incorporated in a Collective Work, but this does not require the Collective Work apart from the Work itself to be made subject to the terms of this Licence. If You create a Collective Work, upon notice from any Licencor You must, to the extent practicable, remove from the Collective Work any reference to such Licensor or the Original Author, as requested.
    b   You may not exercise any of the rights granted to You in Section 3 above in any manner that is primarily intended for or directed toward commercial advantage or private monetary

compensation. The exchange of the Work for other copyrighted works by means of digital file-sharing or otherwise shall not be considered to be intended for or directed toward commercial advantage or private monetary compensation, provided there is no payment of any monetary compensation in connection with the exchange of copyrighted works.

**c** If you distribute, publicly display, publicly perform, or publicly digitally perform the Work or any Collective Works, You must keep intact all copyright notices for the Work and give the Original Author credit reasonable to the medium or means You are utilizing by conveying the name (or pseudonym if applicable) of the Original Author if supplied; the title of the Work if supplied. Such credit may be implemented in any reasonable manner; provided, however, that in the case of a Collective Work, at a minimum such credit will appear where any other comparable authorship credit appears and in a manner at least as prominent as such other comparable authorship credit.

**5. Representations, Warranties and Disclaimer**

**a** By offering the Work for public release under this Licence, Licensor represents and warrants that, to the best of Licensor's knowledge after reasonable inquiry:

**i** Licensor has secured all rights in the Work necessary to grant the licence rights hereunder and to permit the lawful exercise of the rights granted hereunder without␣You having any obligation to pay any royalties, compulsory licence fees, residuals or any other payments;

**ii** The Work does not infringe the copyright, trademark, publicity rights, common law rights or any other right of any third party or constitute defamation, invasion of privacy or other tortious injury to any third party.

**b** EXCEPT AS EXPRESSLY STATED IN THIS LICENCE OR OTHERWISE AGREED IN WRITING OR REQUIRED BY APPLICABLE LAW, THE WORK IS LICENCED ON AN "AS IS" BASIS, WITHOUT WARRANTIES OF ANY KIND, EITHER EXPRESS OR IMPLIED INCLUDING, WITHOUT LIMITATION, ANY WARRANTIES REGARDING THE CONTENTS OR ACCURACY OF THE WORK.

**6. Limitation on Liability.** EXCEPT TO THE EXTENT REQUIRED BY APPLICABLE LAW, AND EXCEPT FOR DAMAGES ARISING FROM LIABILITY TO A THIRD PARTY RESULTING FROM BREACH OF THE WARRANTIES IN SECTION 5, IN NO EVENT WILL LICENSOR BE LIABLE TO YOU ON ANY LEGAL THEORY FOR ANY SPECIAL, INCIDENTAL, CONSEQUENTIAL, PUNITIVE OR EXEMPLARY DAMAGES ARISING OUT OF THIS LICENCE OR THE USE OF THE WORK, EVEN IF LICENSOR HAS BEEN ADVISED OF THE POSSIBILITY OF SUCH DAMAGES.

**7. Termination**

**a** This Licence and the rights granted hereunder will terminate automatically upon any breach by You of the terms of this Licence. Individuals or entities who have received Collective Works from You under this Licence, however, will not have their licences terminated provided such individuals or entities remain in full compliance with those licences. Sections 1, 2, 5, 6, 7, and 8 will survive any termination of this Licence.

**b** Subject to the above terms and conditions, the licence granted here is perpetual (for the duration of the applicable copyright in the Work). Notwithstanding the above, Licensor reserves the right to release the Work under different licence terms or to stop distributing the Work at any time; provided, however that any such election will not serve to withdraw this Licence (or any other licence that has been, or is required to be, granted under the terms of this Licence), and this Licence will continue in full force and effect unless terminated as stated above.

8. Miscellaneous

**a** Each time You distribute or publicly digitally perform the Work or a Collective Work, DEMOS offers to the recipient a licence to the Work on the same terms and conditions as the licence granted to You under this Licence.

**b** If any provision of this Licence is invalid or unenforceable under applicable law, it shall not affect the validity or enforceability of the remainder of the terms of this Licence, and without further action by the parties to this agreement, such provision shall be reformed to the minimum extent necessary to make such provision valid and enforceable.

**c** No term or provision of this Licence shall be deemed waived and no breach consented to unless such waiver or consent shall be in writing and signed by the party to be charged with such waiver or consent.

**d** This Licence constitutes the entire agreement between the parties with respect to the Work licensed here. There are no understandings, agreements or representations with respect to the Work not specified here. Licensor shall not be bound by any additional provisions that may appear in any communication from You. This Licence may not be modified without the mutual written agreement of DEMOS and You.